Here's How

Get Hired Today!

Here's How

Get Hired Today!

GEORGE KENT

NTC LEARNINGWORKS

NTC/Contemporary Publishing Group

Library of Congress Cataloging-in-Publication Data
is available from the United States Library of Congress.

Cover design by Kim Bartko
Cover illustration by Art Glazer
This edition first published in 1991 by VGM Career Horizons

Published by NTC LearningWorks
A division of NTC/Contemporary Publishing Group, Inc.
4255 West Touhy Avenue, Lincolnwood (Chicago), Illinois 60712-1975 U.S.A.
Copyright © 1989 by Copp Clark Pitman
Printed in the United States of America
International Standard Book Number: 0-8442-2949-0

99 00 01 02 03 04 VP 19 18 17 16 15 14 13 12 11 10 9 8 7 6 5 4 3 2 1

About the Author

George E. Kent is the president of Jorge Management Corporation, a Canada-based human resource company sublicensed by Bernard Haldane Associates to provide career management services and outplacement counseling to corporate clients and individuals. Bernard Haldane Associates is the oldest and one of the largest career management services in the world with offices throughout the United States, Canada, and overseas.

Mr. Kent is also chairperson of JMC Recruitment Canada, a subsidiary company of Jorge Management Corporation specializing in recruitment and executive search.

Prior to founding Jorge Management Corporation in 1984, Mr. Kent held executive positions in human resource management and personnel with several national and international companies. His background includes education through the Universities of Manitoba and Winnipeg as well as Queen's University in Kingston, Ontario, and work experience in a wide variety of industries including retailing, wholesaling, manufacturing, insurance, health care, and government.

Mr. Kent is active in many organizations including the Chamber of Commerce, Sales and Marketing Executives, and the Association of Trade and Commerce, and has sat on the board of directors for such groups as Junior Achievement Sales, Marketing Executives, and Job Finding Clubs.

Mr. Kent's main interest, however, is to assist individuals privately or through organizations in finding meaningful employment that will produce the end result of a PERFECT FIT for both the employee and the employer. He has traveled and visited many companies and schools where he lectures in this skill, using his many years of "hands-on experience" to help his audience understand the thinking and expectations of employers.

Mr. Kent will be producing a training video package in this subject area to complement this book and to help educators and social agencies run their own job search programs and clubs. Information on this training video can be obtained by writing to Copp Clark Pitman.

Contents

Introduction

For most people finding a job is very difficult. When you consider the time and effort that *must* be invested in order to be successful, you realize that job hunting can be a full-time job.

Effective job hunting is one of the least developed skills. Personnel work in this area with people from all different educational levels, careers, and positions shows this to be true. As our society becomes increasingly complex, the easy-to-find jobs seem to disappear from the market. Jobs are still there but it takes considerable effort and skill to find them. That is what this book is all about.

The objective of this book is to assist you in the preparation of your own job search program using the proven and effective system suggested. The goal is for YOU to find a job that meets YOUR personal expectations and wants. It is assumed that you have already made a decision regarding your career path and know the type of job for which you are looking. However, if you are unsure about your choice of career or still confused by the vast job choices available today, it is suggested that you first consult a professional career counsellor for testing and guidance.

The detailed method for undertaking a successful job search program is now about to be unfolded in this book. Get ready for a rewarding experience!

1
Getting Organized

1 Getting Organized

Supplies and Equipment

In life, planning is essential for any major undertaking. Preparation before starting is extremely important to the outcome of an event.

Strategies must be planned with sufficient materials; back-up and alternate plans must be tested and made ready to be used when needed. Large successful organizations have plans for today and tomorrow. They know *where* and *how* to make their next move.

Job hunting is no different. You must be prepared in advance for the process you are going to use and have available the materials you will need to support your activities. Before you can start, you will need to set up your own home office with the following essential supplies and tools. Some of them may seem elementary, but they are all basic necessities for a successful job hunt. Have on hand:

- Chair and table or desk in a quiet room away from distractions
- Supply of newsprint writing pads
- Pens, pencils, ruler, highlighters, and postage stamps
- Dictionary and thesaurus
- Quality, letter-size, white bond paper and envelopes
- Lined filing cards and file box
- File folders
- Large appointment/date book
- Pocket-size memo book
- City telephone directory and city road map
- Typewriter or personal computer

In case you're hesitating over that last line on the above list, remember that it's absolutely a *must* to have your résumé and all application letters neatly typed. If you have the resources, also consider obtaining the following:

- Telephone answering machine
- Executive portfolio or briefcase

The telephone answering machine is an excellent investment. You cannot be in two places at the same time. If you're going to make the best use of time on your job search, you cannot sit at home and wait for the phone to ring. Businesses will leave a short message on your machine if your outgoing announcement message is clear and not too lengthy. Once you have made use of this service for business purposes, you will probably wish to use its convenience for social calls also.

The last suggestion is a portfolio in which to carry your résumé into interviews. Employers don't want to see applicants carrying ''bags and bundles'' into the interview as they assume they are full of unnecessary, time-consuming paperwork. A clean and simple portfolio may indicate a tidy personality that ''has it all together.''

2

Identifying Your Skills

2 Identifying Your Skills

Very few people will buy *any* item if they don't know what they're buying. Therefore, salespersons spend considerable time learning about their products in order to present them effectively. In your job search, *you* are the product. So in order to sell a positive image of yourself to employers, you must first know your own particular skills—both your personal qualities and your vocational abilities.

It's also very important to know what employers generally expect from their employees. Then if your skills and the expectations of a prospective employer match, you have an excellent chance of getting the job.

Employer Expectations

Let's begin by looking at things from the employer's side. If you were about to become the owner of a company or the manager of a large firm, what would you expect from your employees?

To answer that question, complete the *Chart of Employer Expectations* on page 9. Assume that the behavior of your employees could have a direct effect on your business and your personal or social life-style. Try to analyze the type of positive behavior you would require. Be as realistic as possible.

When you've come up with a list of ten personal qualities you would require in your employees, number those qualities in priority order. Try to match the order you consider most employers would adopt.

A *Chart of Employer Expectations* is shown filled in for you on page 11. Do you agree with the priority ordering of the qualities in this example? Would you include any of these qualities in your own chart?

You will discover that filling out this chart can be a very valuable exercise. Once you start thinking like management in this matter, you will have a better understanding of the questions interviewers will ask and the signs of positive behavior they will be looking for in your answers. Then it will be up to you to convey by your remarks that you *do* have the personal qualities most required by employers. Interviewers may not express their approval outwardly; but they will mentally note your comments—to your advantage.

Chart of Employee Expectations

Condition Expected   **Priority Order**

1. _____

2. _____

3. _____

4. _____

5. _____

6. _____

7. _____

8. _____

9. _____

10. _____

Chart of Employer Expectations—Sample

	Quality Expected	Priority Order
1.	hard-working	2
2.	loyal	1
3.	polite	10
4.	honest	6
5.	punctual	4
6.	creative	9
7.	compatible	8
8.	reliable	3
9.	accurate	5
10.	organized	7

Employee Skills

Now let's turn to the subject of knowing your own particular skills. In building your list of skills, you should consider both your accomplishments and the positive experiences you have had over the past several years. These experiences are important in identifying your skills whether they happened at school, at home, at work, or in your social life.

Generally speaking, skills can be divided into qualities and abilities— what you're like and what you can do. The exercises that follow will help you to identify both types of skill.

Identifying Your Personal Qualities

As already discussed, employers consider positive behavior characteristics—good personal qualities—to be vitally important. These qualities are the strengths which distinguish excellent employees. Which of these strengths do you possess?

The *Chart of Personal Qualities* provided here will help you to find out. After looking at the filled-in sample shown on page 14, turn to the blank chart given on page 15. First, write your own name where indicated; then, make several photocopies of the chart.

On your own copy, check off or add those qualities which *you* consider describe you best. Next, hand out fresh copies to your relatives and friends. This time, ask these other people to check off or add those qualities which *they* consider describe you best.

Compare the results. Does your self-image match the way you appear to others? This can be a very interesting exercise!

To identify those characteristics which are really your three top strengths, collate the results from all the copies. Choose as your first top strength the quality checked off or added the most times. Choose your second and third top strengths by the same method.

After you have identified your three top strengths, take each one and write a short paragraph on your experience in using this strength. This will help to reinforce your belief that you really possess the strength in question. Then, on a scale of 1-10 identify the importance of each strength or characteristic as it describes the "real" you.

Learn to use these characteristic top strengths as positive selling points about yourself. If you talk about them enough and become convinced that these really *are* your top strengths, you will be able to project that conviction in your responses at interviews.

Identifying Your Vocational Abilities

It's also important to identify your specific job skills—the things you can do well and the areas in which you can function effectively.

Various tasks are described in the *Chart of Vocational Abilities* given on page 16. Read through this chart and check off all those functions which you feel you can perform expertly or adequately. If you feel you are skilled at other functions not included in this list, add these functions in the space provided.

From among the things which you can do expertly, choose those three functions in which you show the greatest skill. Rate these functions as your first, second, and third main skills, as shown on the sample chart which has been filled in for you on page 17.

If you were unable to check off three functions in the "Expertly" column, choose some or all of your three main skills from the "Adequately" column. Then prepare a short list on each of your three main skills. State how long you have possessed each skill, where you learned it, and where you have used it.

As you work through this exercise, be careful not to interpret the functions too strictly. Take, for example, the function ''Teach others.'' At first glance, you might say to yourself: ''I don't have a degree in Education. I'm not a teacher. I can't check off this function.''

Consider, however, that you may have been very successful at training your fellow workers in special job procedures; or at training your friends or fellow club members in skilled handicraft methods. In these situations, you *have* been able to ''teach others''; and all such life experiences make up the total package of skills which you can bring to the job market. By looking at the skills exercise in this way, you will probably discover that you can check off many more functions than you might have thought possible.

Chart of Personal Qualities—Sample

Name: *Mai Nguyen*

Instructions: From the list below, check off those qualities which you consider best describe the person named above. If you feel this person possesses other qualities not included in this list, add these qualities in the space provided.

☑ accurate	☐ economical	☐ perceptive
☐ adventurous	☐ efficient	☐ persevering
☐ affectionate	☐ emotional	☐ persuasive
☐ aggressive	☐ flexible	☑ polite
☐ alert	☐ foresighted	☐ practical
☐ ambitious	☐ generous	☐ professional
☐ artistic	☐ gentle	☐ progressive
☐ assertive	☑ hard-working	☑ punctual
☐ cautious	☑ honest	☑ reliable
☐ charming	☐ humorous	☐ reserved
☑ compatible	☐ imaginative	☐ risk-taking
☐ competent	☐ inventive	☐ scientific
☐ competitive	☐ investigative	☐ sensitive
☐ conscientious	☐ logical	☐ sincere
☐ conservative	☑ loyal	☐ spontaneous
☐ considerate	☐ mature	☐ sympathetic
☐ creative	☐ open-minded	☐ thorough
☐ dependable	☑ organized	☐ thoughtful
☐ discreet	☐ outgoing	☐ understanding

Other Qualities: *tactful*

Chart of Personal Qualities

Name: _____

Instructions: From the list below, check off those qualities which you consider best describe the person named above. If you feel this person possesses other qualities not included in this list, add these qualities in the space provided.

☐ accurate	☐ economical	☐ perceptive
☐ adventurous	☐ efficient	☐ persevering
☐ affectionate	☐ emotional	☐ persuasive
☐ aggressive	☐ flexible	☐ polite
☐ alert	☐ foresighted	☐ practical
☐ ambitious	☐ generous	☐ professional
☐ artistic	☐ gentle	☐ progressive
☐ assertive	☐ hard-working	☐ punctual
☐ cautious	☐ honest	☐ reliable
☐ charming	☐ humorous	☐ reserved
☐ compatible	☐ imaginative	☐ risk-taking
☐ competent	☐ inventive	☐ scientific
☐ competitive	☐ investigative	☐ sensitive
☐ conscientious	☐ logical	☐ sincere
☐ conservative	☐ loyal	☐ spontaneous
☐ considerate	☐ mature	☐ sympathetic
☐ creative	☐ open-minded	☐ thorough
☐ dependable	☐ organized	☐ thoughtful
☐ discreet	☐ outgoing	☐ understanding

Other Qualities: _____

_____

Chart of Vocational Abilities

Expertly	Adequately	I am able to:	
☐	☐	Analyze reports	☐
☐	☐	Compose correspondence	☐
☐	☐	Cook meals	☐
☐	☐	Coordinate functions	☐
☐	☐	Do liaison work	☐
☐	☐	Do mechanical tasks	☐
☐	☐	Follow through on projects	☐
☐	☐	Function as a team player	☐
☐	☐	Generate ideas	☐
☐	☐	Guard property	☐
☐	☐	Initiate plans	☐
☐	☐	Input data	☐
☐	☐	Lead groups	☐
☐	☐	Meet deadlines	☐
☐	☐	Negotiate agreements	☐
☐	☐	Observe systems	☐
☐	☐	Organize material	☐
☐	☐	Plan activities	☐
☐	☐	Prepare budgets	☐
☐	☐	Remember facts	☐
☐	☐	Select options	☐
☐	☐	Sell merchandise	☐
☐	☐	Speak at meetings	☐
☐	☐	Supervise children	☐
☐	☐	Take care of details	☐
☐	☐	Teach others	☐
☐	☐	Work with numbers	☐
☐	☐	Write articles	☐
☐	☐	_____	☐
☐	☐	_____	☐
☐	☐	_____	☐

Chart of Vocational Abilities—Sample

Expertly	Adequately	I am able to:	
☐	☐	Analyze reports	☐
☐	☐	Compose correspondence	☐
☐	☐	Cook meals	☐
☐	☐	Coordinate functions	☐
☐	☑	Do liaison work	☐
☑	☐	Do mechanical tasks	☐
☐	☑	Follow through on projects	☐
☐	☑	Function as a team player	☐
☐	☐	Generate ideas	☐
☐	☐	Guard property	☐
☐	☐	Initiate plans	☐
☐	☐	Input data	☐
☐	☐	Lead groups	☐
☐	☐	Meet deadlines	☐
☐	☐	Negotiate agreements	☐
☐	☐	Observe systems	☐
☐	☑	Organize material	☐
☐	☐	Plan activities	☐
☐	☐	Prepare budgets	☐
☐	☑	Remember facts	☐
☐	☐	Select options	☐
☐	☐	Sell merchandise	☐
☐	☐	Speak at meetings	☐
☐	☐	Supervise children	☐
☑	☐	Take care of details	☑
☑	☐	Teach others	☑
☑	☐	Work with numbers	☑
☐	☐	Write articles	☐
☑	☐	*File records* _____	☐
☐	☐	_____	☐
☐	☐	_____	☐

3

Selling Yourself on Paper

3 Selling Yourself on Paper

Preparing Your Résumé

A résumé is a *summary* of one's education, skills, employment history, and pertinent personal information. The objective of a résumé is to provide sufficient information to awaken the reader's interest. It should make the reader want to receive *more* information but *through an interview*. A résumé will not, by itself, get you a job offer.

Most people have a tendency to describe in detail all the duties and responsibilities of every job they have ever had. They also list schools, grades, and subjects taken at junior levels. A well-traveled person who had worked for 30 years could write a novel-length résumé by detailing everything!

The longer your résumé is, the greater the risk that it will not be understood or even read entirely. Competition for good jobs results in a high volume of résumés and applications. It takes a trained, well-disciplined interviewer to give the same consideration to the last application as to the first. Professional systems are available to help ensure that all candidates are treated fairly but, in fact, many companies operate without such systems.

Another mistake many people make—even those who claim to be ''professional résumé writers''—is to detail information that is protected under human rights legislation. Human rights legislation restricts employers from demanding certain information that might be used to discriminate in making the hiring decision. Then why should you freely provide this information? Equal Opportunity Employment Commission provides guidelines to employers regarding questions and information that must be avoided. You will find it to your advantage to follow these same guidelines in preparing your résumé.

Rules for Résumés

The following list of suggested rules should prove helpful to you in the preparation of your résumé.

1. Present your résumé in a clear, well-laid-out manner, on quality white paper. Do not use ''gimmick'' paper, colors, or styles.

Although you might think such attention-getters would be to your advantage, they could be looked upon as attempts to influence the employer and the résumé could be rejected because of them.

2. Type your résumé.

3. Do not date your résumé.

4. Put your career goal near the beginning. Since many people "scan" down the résumé, it is important that you "grab" their attention right away.

5. Keep your résumé neat and brief. If possible limit it to two pages. Use headings to list information. Compress lengthy sentences into short statements. Your résumé will be easier to read and understand if it is concise.

6. Do not make mistakes in spelling or grammar. If you're applying for a secretarial job such mistakes could be disastrous! These kinds of errors make your résumé look unprofessional and spoil your chance to make a good first impression.

7. Be honest. No one wants to hire someone who lies or exaggerates. Your résumé must accurately recap your background. You may not change the fact that you performed certain duties during an employment period. You may not change the dates either. When employers uncover the smallest of "errors," they then become cautious about the remaining information.

8. Do not make "negative statements." Any information that indicates you do not have the standard of quality wanted by employers will prompt them to continue their search by looking elsewhere. You cannot lie but you don't have to give away "handicaps" that have no relationship or connection to the job for which you are applying. This is *very important* as employers make their final decisions based on the total amount of negative information they obtain in the whole screening process.

9. Do not include your salary requirements. Some employers may consider that you are "too expensive." Others may consider that your stated requirements are "too low." As a result, they may assume that your skills are not sufficient to do the job. If you are specifically asked to state your salary expectations for a particular job, put them in a covering letter.

10. Do not include references. If you are asked to provide references, list them in your covering letter. Choose as references business acquaintances who know your work behavior.

11. Do not include your picture. If you are applying for a position where the employer can *legally* ask for your picture, then attach the picture to your covering letter. Human rights legislation protects

applicants from discrimination based on sex, race, or age. Your picture will give this information.

12.   Carry your résumé in a portfolio or briefcase in order to keep its pages clean and fresh-looking in appearance—another good impression!

Skills in Your Résumé

Through the charts in the last chapter, you identified your outstanding strengths and skills. Now it's very important to transfer this information to your résumé.

Under the résumé heading "Personal Characteristics," list those characteristics which you checked off in your *Chart of Personal Qualities*. Be sure to include those you identified as your three top strengths. If possible, also include those qualities to which you gave first priority in your *Chart of Employer Expectations*.

Under the résumé heading "Work History," give instances where you have performed the functions checked off in your *Chart of Vocational Abilities*. Concentrate especially on those functions which you identified as your three main skills. Also include these skills in your remarks under the résumé heading "Career Goal."

Your Covering Letter

A covering letter is a *must* for any résumé. It's the introduction to your résumé—the attention-grabber!

Covering letters must always be originals for every individual position applied for. Photocopied "general" covering letters, with "specific" inserts aimed at a particular job, are definitely a mistake. They indicate that you could not take the time to compose a letter that applied to the job in question. Instead, you expected the interviewer to read through all of your material and sort out what applied to that particular job. Letters like this make a very poor first impression!

If possible, address your covering letter to an individual, using the *correct* spelling of the person's name and title. Using the form of address "Dear Sir or Madam" shows that you were not willing to spend the time and effort needed to secure the name of the *appropriate* company contact.

Your letter should be clean and neat, with *no errors*. "White-out" is not acceptable. Type the letter over again!

Try not to go beyond one page in length. In the first paragraph, indicate why you are writing and what source of information led you to contact this company.

In the second paragraph, tell about your education and/or experience and how these relate to the open position. This paragraph should be your "hook." Stress the part of your background that would be a definite asset to the company to which you're writing. This hooks your reader's interest.

Finish by suggesting or, more assertively, by *telling* the reader that you will telephone to arrange an interview so that you may provide additional information about yourself. Tell the reader the date you will call; then mark that date on your calendar and make sure to follow through as promised.

Sample Résumés

On the following pages, several sample résumés are presented as examples of the points that have been discussed. Take the time to study these résumés carefully. You will find them very useful as models when you start to prepare your own résumé.

The final résumé sample, the one for Carl Braun, also has a sample of a covering letter to go along with it. Again, study the techniques shown by this letter, which you will find on page 38. Then, as a practice exercise for yourself, write samples of covering letters to accompany each of the other résumés used as examples. This will be a good learning experience that will help you to prepare your own *real* covering letters later on.

MAI NGUYEN
401 Riverdale Avenue
New York, NY 12180

(315) 555-8300

CAREER GOAL

To work for small office with opportunity for promotion to an accounting supervisory position where I can use my skills at figures and training others.

PERSONAL
CHARACTERISTICS

Loyal, hard-working, reliable, polite

EDUCATION

College of the City of New York
Convent Avenue, West 139th Street, New York, NY 10031

Degree in Business Studies, 1986
(Two-year program with emphasis on accounting)

Moss Park High School
637 Ardmore Place, New York, NY 13208

High School Graduation, 1984

WORK HISTORY

June 1986 to present

OFFICE CLERK at Gulf and Western Investment Counselors, Inc.
Gulf and Western Plaza, New York NY 10023

Supervisor: Mrs. Anne Rutherford, (555-6448)

I have handled a variety of duties with Gulf and Western, including accounts payable, accounts receivable, payroll, and filing. For the past year, I have helped Mrs. Rutherford train new employees to do commission calculations for payroll. Just recently, I have become responsible for collating all the details needed to prepare the month-end accounting reports.

PERSONAL DATA

Willing to work overtime

HOBBIES/
INTERESTS

Interpretive dancing, embroidery, cooking, calligraphy

REFERENCES

Available on request

ANTONIO DONATELLI
90 Lakeshore Road
Melrose Park, IL 60160

(708) 555-0443

CAREER GOAL	To work for a responsible company in a position where I can use my training and past experience in kitchen support and commercial food cooking
PERSONAL CHARACTERISTICS	Dependable, honest, hard-working, friendly
PERSONAL DATA	Willing to work shifts
EDUCATION	Cooking and Hospitality Institute of Chicago, Inc. 361 W. Chestnut, Chicago, IL 60610
	Commercial Food Preparation Certificate, 1988 (Three-year program)
	Fort Richmond High School 1641 McKay Street, Melrose Park, IL 60164
	High School Graduation, 1985
WORK HISTORY	September 1987 to present
	DIETARY AID (part-time) at Gottlieb Hospital 8700 W. North Avenue, Melrose Park, IL 60160
	Supervisor: Mr. Luc Rivest (555-0041)
	While working at the hospital, I have been assigned to various duties in the Dietary Department. Most of my responsibilities have involved working in the food line and doing clean-up after the meal periods. I have assisted in serving meals both to hospital employees and to visitors. Recently, I have also begun helping in the auxiliary kitchen, preparing salads and evening snacks.

ANTONIO DONATELLI
Page 2

**WORK HISTORY
CONTINUED**

June 8, 1987 to August 12, 1987

DISHWASHER at Anne's Kitchen
1220 Euclid Avenue, Oak Park, IL 60302

Owner: Mrs. W. Landowski (555-5826)

This was a school work-experience assignment for the month of June, and
then a summer job until I went on vacation with my family. I liked working at
the Kitchen, but I gave up the job because the distance was too far to travel
by bus for weekend and evening work.

January 12, 1985 to June 5, 1987

COOK at McDonald's Restaurant
1314 Hood Avenue, Melrose Park, IL 60160

Manager: Mr. V. Omer (555-7688)

I really enjoyed the 2 1/2 years I spent at McDonald's. I worked in almost
every position at the restaurant. I left in order to have a different work
experience in another type of restaurant.

**HOBBIES/
INTERESTS**

Cooking, model building, cycling, sports

REFERENCES

Available on request

LEAH CONE
35 Melrose Avenue, Apt. 212
Greenville, SC 29611

(803) 555-0445

CAREER GOAL

To work for a large, well-organized insurance company where I can use my present skills and find opportunities for advancement

PERSONAL
CHARACTERISTICS

Loyal, punctual, reliable

PERSONAL DATA

Willing to travel

EDUCATION

University of South Carolina
Columbia, SC 29208

2nd Year Arts, 1987

Seaforth High School
21 Delta Drive, Greenville, SC 29609

High School Graduation, 1985

WORK HISTORY

May 1987 to June 1988

INSURANCE ADMINISTRATION CLERK at J.W. Howard and Associates, Inc.
221 N. Main, Greenville, SC 29601

President: Mr. Jerome Howard (555-2445)

I held the only clerical position in the company. I was responsible for helping the agents with their call reports, new sales, and claims for damages or lost property. I provided all the keyboarding to the computer, did the invoicing for new policies and renewals, and gathered information for the biweekly commission checks.

September 1985 to April 1987

DESK CLERK at the Lipton Motor Hotel
3490 Rocky Point, Columbia, SC 29208

Manager: Ms. L. Chung (555-3034)

I worked part time at the Lipton while attending the University of South Carolina.

LEAH CONE
Page 2

HOBBIES/
INTERESTS   Water sports, flying, entertaining, classical music, decorating

ASSOCIATIONS   Member of the University of South Carolina debating team

                         President of my high school graduation committee

                         Member of the community center swim club

REFERENCES   Available on request

FIDEL RAMIREZ
847 Grace Street
Berkeley, CA 94720

(619) 555-2180

CAREER GOAL   To work for a well-known newspaper where I can use my skills and experience in writing, photography, and sports

PERSONAL
CHARACTERISTICS   Hard-working, dependable, loyal

PERSONAL DATA   Willing to work overtime

EDUCATION   University of California
714 University Hall, Berkeley, CA 94720

Level 2 of the program leading to the Creative Writing Certificate completed, June 1988

David Hall High School
14 Acoma Avenue, San Diego, CA 92117

High School Graduation, 1986

SKILLS TRANING   St. John Ambulance
2625 Byrd Street, Berkeley, CA 94701

CPR Certificate, March 1988

WORK HISTORY   October 1986 to present

NEWSROOM ASSISTANT at the *Mid City Post*
P.O. Box 2220, Berkeley, CA 94776

Editor: Mr. Daniel Tarasko (555-2920)

I work part time at the *Post*, on weekends and holidays, assisting at the city desk and helping the reporters.

FIDEL RAMIREZ
Page 2

HOBBIES/
INTERESTS   Photography, basketball, racket sports, reading

ASSOCIATIONS   President of my high school photo club

                         Assistant coach of the senior basketball team

                         Member of my high school yearbook committee

                         Instructor in table tennis at the community center

REFERENCES   Available on request

MARIKA JANIC
32 Crestland Avenue, Apt. 412
New Orleans, LA 70107

(318) 555-2297

CAREER GOAL

To find a responsible position with a respected firm where I can use my education and experience to help the company reach its objectives

PERSONAL
CHARACTERISTICS

Outgoing, compatible, loyal, hard-working, dependable

PERSONAL DATA

Willing to travel
Willing to move

EDUCATION

Tulane University
6823 St. Charles Avenue, New Orleans, LA 70118

Bachelor of Arts, 1984
(Major, psychology)

Jones High School
91 Midway Street, Lafayette, LA 70501

High School Graduation, 1980

SKILLS TRANING

Public Speaking
7-hour program, December 1987
JMC Group Management

Recruitment, The Whole Picture
2-day program, October 1987
Human Resource Systems

Assertiveness Training
10 sessions, April 1986
Delgado College
615 City Park Avenue, New Orleans, LA 70119

MARIKA JANIC
Page 2

VOCATIONAL
ABILITIES

I have the following business skills:
- Keyboarding (85 wpm)
- Dictaphone
- Payroll
- Intermediate accounting
- Lotus 1-2-3 spreadsheet software
- Word Perfect word processing software
- Page Maker desktop publishing software

WORK HISTORY

January 1987 to present

OFFICE SUPERVISOR at Arrow Enterprises, Inc.
12 Lloyd Road, New Orleans, LA 70106

Manager: Mr. Mavrin (555-4120)

My duties include:
- Coordinating all office support activities
- Hiring, training and evaluating office staff
- Providing all month-end reports to the manager
- Ensuring information is sent to all clients

July 1984 to December 1986

OFFICE CLERK at United Insurance Agencies
211 Monticello Drive, New Orleans, LA 70111

Supervisor: Ms. Roberti (555-2884)

In this position, I:
- Provided keyboarding support for agents
- Processed payroll
- Supervised part-time clerks

HOBBIES/
INTERESTS

Computers, reading, sports, sewing, outdoor activities

ASSOCIATIONS

Volunteer at Metro General Hospital
Member of church fund-raising committee

REFERENCES

Available on request

JEAN PERRAULT
332 Roberval Street
Jacksonville, FL 32219

(904) 555-2248

CAREER GOALS

To work in a large retail store where I can train to become a supervisor

PERSONAL
CHARACTERISTICS

Very easy to get along with, reliable, well-mannered

PERSONAL DATA

Completely bilingual in English and French
Willing to work shifts

EDUCATION

Atlantic Heights High School
49061 Channel Road, Jacksonville, FL 32244
High School Graduation, 1988

SKILLS TRAINING

Technology Institute
21 Piper Drive, Jacksonville, FL 32207
Stereo Technology, Level B, 1988

Brookfield Academy of Music
1600 San Rae Road, Jacksonville, FL 32217

Grade 9 Guitar, 1987

WORK HISTORY

September 1984 to June 1988

CLERK at Perrault's Men's Wear
284 Normandie Street, Jacksonville, FL 32219

Owner: M.René Perrault (555-4921)

While at high school, I worked part time in my uncle's clothing store.
My responsibilities included:
• Receiving shipments, pricing goods, and stocking shelves
• Helping customers
• Acting as cashier

JEAN PERRAULT
Page 2

HOBBIES/
INTERESTS   Playing guitar and drums, collect CD records

ASSOCIATIONS   Member of "Impose" pop-rock group
                     Class vice-president in Grade 12

REFERENCES   Available on request

BARBARA JANE O'MALLEY
143 Caribou Road
Sioux Falls, SD 57103
(605) 555-4522

CAREER GOAL   To continue with my high school education and then study to become a veterinarian

PERSONAL
CHARACTERISTICS   Punctual, well-groomed, polite

PERSONAL DATA   Like to cook

EDUCATION   Sam Douglas High School
                     23 Maryknoll Drive, Sioux Falls, SD 57105

                     Sophomore year completed, June 1988

WORK HISTORY   May 1987 to present
                     COOK'S HELPER (part-time) at Grandma Leigh's Dining Room
                     45 Pinegrove Avenue, Sioux Falls, SD 57103

                     Owner: Mrs. Augusta Leigh (555-0343)

                     I work approximately 12 hours per week in the kitchen. My duties are:
                     • Washing dishes and cooking utensils
                     • Making salads and cutting vegetables
                     • Cooking hamburgers and making sandwiches
                     • Cleaning kitchen at the end of my shift

HOBBIES/
INTERESTS   Animal grooming, reading, collecting stuffed toys, sports, dancing, cheerleading

REFERENCES   Available on request

CARL BRAUN
987 Jefferson Avenue, Apt. 112
Detroit, MI 48234
(313) 555-4318

CAREER GOAL

To be part of a supervisory team whose objective is to manufacture a specific product with emphasis on quality control and overall productivity

PERSONAL
CHARACTERISTICS

Self-motivated, creative, assertive

PERSONAL DATA

Willing to relocate and/or travel
Speak and write English, German, and French

QUALIFICATIONS

Industrial Engineering degree

Creative/investigative problem-solving experience

Work-flow design background

Leadership ability, with skill in developing team participation

ACHIEVEMENTS

Developed a production route to eliminate over-handling of product and cut labor time, thereby reducing costs by 38 percent and increasing company profits

Cross-trained staff to increase productivity and reduce absenteeism, with resulting payroll savings of $150,000 per year

EXPERIENCE

October 1986 to present

INDUSTRIAL ENGINEER at AIF Manufacturing, Inc.
417 Jackson Avenue, Detroit, MI 48210

Plant Manager: Mr. Paul Miki (555-0429)

Already in this position, I have:
• Coordinated plant reorganization team
• Developed training methods for shop supervisors
• Made the significant contributions listed above under the heading "Achievements"

CARL BRAUN
Page 2

EXPERIENCE
CONTINUED

July 1985 to September 1986

QUALITY CONTROL INSPECTOR at Reman Enterprises Inc.
1993 Hastings Street, Detroit, MI 48211

Owner: Mr. Albert Reman (555-6041)

At Reman Enterprises, I:
• Inspected new products for defects
• Trained plant workers to use mechanical test equipment
• Recommended new methods of inspection

EDUCATION

University of Illinois
750 South Halsted, Chicago, Il 60607
Degree in Industrial Engineering, 1985

Devry Institute of Technology
3300 North Campbell Avenue, Chicago, IL 60618
Computer Management Systems Diploma, 1981

SKILLS TRAINING

Professional Supervisory Techniques
Weekend seminar, November 1986
Industry Consultants, Inc.
8883 Barnet Road, Detroit, MI 48211

HOBBIES/
INTERESTS

Public speaking, sailing, horseback riding, wilderness survival trips

ASSOCIATIONS

Chairperson of the district Toastmasters Club

Secretary of the "Ancient Mariner" tall ships club

Member of the "Adventure North" camping club

REFERENCES

Available on request

987 Jefferson Avenue, Apt. 112
Detroit, MI 48234
July 20, 19--

Mr. Sam Grundy, Chief Engineer
Float Bio-Gem Inc.
99 2nd Avenue
Detroit, MI 48210

Dear Mr. Grundy:

When I was speaking recently with Otto Werner, he suggested that I contact you regarding your plans to hire an engineering manager next month. As Mr. Werner had worked for you in this capacity last year, he outlined your firm's basic requirements for this management position.

Your Requirements	My Qualifications
• University degree in engineering	• Graduated from the University of Illinois as an industrial engineer • Have a diploma in Computer Management
• Minimum of two year's experience in manufacturing	• One year of experience as a manufacturing quality control inspector • Over two years of experience as an industrial engineer in a high-technology manufacturing plant
• Good analytical abilities	• Studied, developed, and installed a new system of product flow and reduced labor costs by 38 percent • Studied a high-absenteeism problem and reduced this problem by installing a job-enrichment program

Realizing that you have a busy schedule, I will call you on Monday, July 27 to arrange a convenient meeting time where I can expand further on my background and on how I feel it will be an asset to your company.

Yours truly,

Carl Braun

Carl Braun

Enc: Résumé

Preparing Your Information Card

In the next chapter, the subject of enlisting a whole network of contacts to help you in your job search will be covered in detail. If these contacts have no information about you, however, how can they answer questions regarding you, or give information to potential employers on your behalf? Obviously, this could be a problem! The solution is to have your own personal information card available to hand out to all your contacts and job prospects.

The information card shown on page 40 has been designed to give sufficient facts about what you have done, where you want to go with your career, and what your positive personal characteristics are. This card is *different*; and because it is, it will make people want to read it and know how it works—*all to your advantage.*

The size of the card makes it convenient to carry and gives it a professional look. Pulling out a dog-eared sheet of paper does not make the kind of impression you want on a contact person or potential employer! On the other hand, using the neat little information card says volumes about your good planning skills and resource materials.

Your completed résumé is the source for your information card. In fact, you might say that your information card is your résumé in a nutshell.

The work history section of your résumé is summed up in the career capsule part of your information card. This career capsule should be very short but it should also be accurate and informative. It should be a thumbnail sketch of what you have done. For example: ''Over two years' sales experience in the garment industry retail field, in increasingly responsible positions dealing with customers and fellow employees.''

The career goal from your résumé is repeated on your information card. This career goal should state where you want to go over the next several years. Most people just want a job and give no thought to tomorrow. Employers want people who can think ahead, plan, and have some direction to their careers. As on your résumé, remember to stress your main skills here on your information card. For example: ''To work for a responsible and professional employer where I can use my excellent people skills in striving hard towards advancement opportunities.''

The personal characteristics given on your résumé are also listed here again on your information card. Since space on the card is limited, be sure to list your top strengths first. As you've already discovered, these personal characteristics are very important because they tell employers what your personal and work habits are. For example: "Honest, dependable, punctual."

A completed information card is shown below as a sample. Blank cards are also provided for your personal use in your own job search. You may photocopy these cards. Or, if you prefer, you may draw up your own information card, based on the printed model. Then prepare as many copies of your card as you wish, using standard-size lined index cards.

Information Card—Sample

Name: *Mai Nguyen*   Phone: *238-8300*

Job wanted: *General accounting clerk*

Career capsule: *Three years' experience with a large service company doing accts. pay., accts. rec., payroll, and filing*

Career goal: *To work in a small office with opportunity for promotion to an accounting supervisory position where I can use my skills at figures and training others*

Personal characteristics: *Loyal, hard-working, reliable, polite*

Information Card

Name: _____ Phone: _____

Job wanted: _____

Career capsule: _____

_____

_____

Career goal: _____

_____

Personal characteristics: _____

_____

_____

Information Card

Name: _____ Phone: _____

Job wanted: _____

Career capsule: _____

_____

_____

Career goal: _____

_____

Personal characteristics: _____

_____

_____

Information Card

Name: _____ Phone: _____

Job wanted: _____

Career capsule: _____

_____

_____

Career goal: _____

_____

Personal characteristics: _____

_____

_____

Information Card

Name: _____ Phone: _____

Job wanted: _____

Career capsule: _____

_____

_____

Career goal: _____

_____

Personal characteristics: _____

_____

_____

4

Establishing Your Contacts

4 Establishing Your Contacts

The "Networking Secret"

Insurance agents, car dealers, and real estate agents all know the importance of a network of contacts. They know that such a network is the secret of success—the first and best way of finding leads for sales.

Using this network system is referred to informally as "networking." In your job search, *"networking" is the process of enlisting other people to help you find employment*. These people will become *your sales agents* to "market" your skills and experience to people they know and to potential employers. Why do it all yourself when you can manage a team of people *committed* to assisting you?

To begin networking, you must find a group of dependable, first-line contact people who will make a commitment to helping you in this program. You must ask these people to talk about your job search to others who, in their turn, will pass on the information to still others, in an ever-widening circle.

News about possible job leads uncovered by any of these people will be passed back through all the circles of the network right to your first-line contact. This first-line person will then pass the information on to you.

The accompanying diagram, *Circle of Contacts*, shows how networking can EXPLODE into dozens of people assisting you to look for work opportunities or leads. Your first-line contact—your next-door neighbor—enlists 3 other second-line contacts. These people then enlist 9 third-line contacts who, in their turn, enlist 27 fourth-line contacts. So from just a single first-line person you gain an additional 39 contacts!

Can you imagine how many contacts you could gain if you had 20 to 45 first-line network people helping you? If you're careful in selecting your first-line contacts—and thorough in explaining to them how the process works and what you're asking them to do—you will have tremendous success with your system.

CIRCLE OF CONTACTS

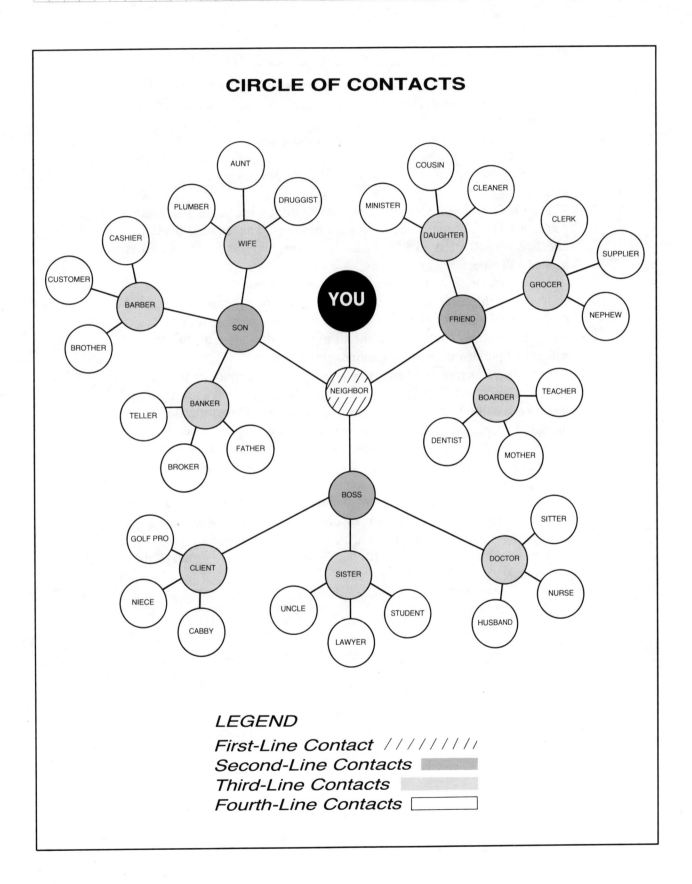

LEGEND

First-Line Contact / / / / / / / /
Second-Line Contacts
Third-Line Contacts
Fourth-Line Contacts

Sources of First-Line Contacts

If the job of *finding* this first group of dependable helpers strikes you as sounding too difficult, don't be discouraged. It's really not as hard as it sounds!

Just take that one large, difficult, general question "Whom shall I ask?" and break it down into many small, easy, specific questions such as "Whom do I invite over to my home?" or "With whom do I travel to work?"

The *Chart of Contact People* given on the following pages will prompt you to ask yourself many such specific questions. This chart is divided into five parts: Part A to Part E. In each part, the left-hand column is headed "Prospects."

As you read each entry printed under the "Prospects" heading, ask yourself, "Whom could this be in my life? Is there a prospective contact here for me?" Several persons that you might otherwise never have thought of will probably then come to mind. Write down all of their names and phone numbers on the lines provided.

Don't leave anyone out because you assume they cannot help. The more ears you have listening and the more mouths you have asking, the less time it will take you to land that important job. Therefore, don't disregard people because you think they are too young, too uneducated, too quiet, or too long away from the job market. Instead, write down the names of everyone you can think of for each entry under "Prospects."

After you have filled in the whole chart, review all the names. Look for people who may be in direct competition with you for a job and remove their names. The names left in the chart will belong to the persons you will now approach for help—your prospective group of first-line contacts.

Chart of Contact People

Part A: Relatives

Prospects	Names	Phone Numbers
Parents:	_____	_____
	_____	_____
Brothers:	_____	_____
	_____	_____
	_____	_____
Sisters:	_____	_____
	_____	_____
	_____	_____
Uncles:	_____	_____
	_____	_____
Aunts:	_____	_____
	_____	_____
Cousins:	_____	_____
	_____	_____
	_____	_____
	_____	_____
In-laws:	_____	_____
	_____	_____
	_____	_____
	_____	_____
Godparents:	_____	_____
	_____	_____

Part B: Friends

Prospects	Names	Phone Numbers
Neighbors:		
Go to same club:		
Go to same church:		
Vacation with:		
Share same hobby:		
Go to their home:		
Invite to my home:		

Part C: Professionals

Prospects	Names	Phone Numbers
Minister:		
Doctor:		
Dentist:		
Lawyer:		
Accountant:		
Banker:		
Politicians:		

Part D: People at School

Prospects	Names	Phone Numbers
Best teachers:		
Special friends:		
Class officers:		
Play sports with:		
Socialize with:		

Part E: People at Work

Prospects	Names	Phone Numbers
Supervisors:		
Go to work with:		
Eat lunch with:		
Socialize with:		
Help me in my job:		
Help in their job:		

Your Personal Contacts File

The next step is to set up a special file for your first-line contacts. To do this, work through all the names in your *Chart of Contact People*, asking for everyone's assistance.

This step can be done in person or over the telephone. In person is perhaps more effective but over the phone is a better use of time at this stage. Cross off your chart any persons who say they're unable to help. Make up an index card for each person who agrees to help you.

An index card especially suited to this purpose—the contact card—has been designed. Blank copies of this card are provided for you at the end of this chapter. For now, however, let's look at a filled-in sample of this special card and go over its details point by point.

Contact Card—Sample

Name: *Aunt Joyce Nguyen*   Phone: *237-0945*

First call: *June 23, 2:00*   Return call: *June 27, 7:30*

☑ Reason for call	☑ Know any owners?
☑ About contact *(Helped with job at Investment Counselor)*	☑ Know of new firms?
☑ Job information	☑ Companies growing?
☑ Being promoted?	☑ Companies hiring?
☑ Being transferred?	☑ Ask relatives?
☑ Retiring/leaving?	☑ Ask acquaintances?
☑ Starting new job?	☑ Ask supervisor?
☑ Getting new boss?	☑ Ask personnel?

Using Contact Cards

The first lines on the card—"Name" and "Phone"—refer to the name and phone number of your contact, obtainable from your *Chart of Contact People*. The "First call" and "Return call" lines give you the space you need to fill in the dates and times of your phone calls. Using the "Return call" line is a *very* important part of the whole system. Using this line will be talked about further at the end of this section.

The rest of the card is made up of reminders with little boxes beside them. Most of these reminders are abbreviated questions. These questions are meant to act as "prompters" that will jog your memory and remind you to ask your contact person all of these things. The boxes are there so that you can check off each question as you ask it.

Without a convenient memory aid like this to help you, it's possible that you might omit a certain question when talking with some contact. That single, forgotten question might refer to the *one* area in which your contact could have helped you! By using contact cards with everyone you speak to about your job search, you can be sure that no important points will be left out of your conversations.

The first three prompters on the card are reminders of a slightly different sort from the rest. ''Reason for call'' reminds you to come straight to the point and do your best to enlist the other person's help in your job search.

''About contact'' may not always apply. However, if your contact has achieved something special or has aided you in the past, this prompter reminds you to say something complimentary about the person's accomplishments or helpfulness. If you do this, your listener will be pleased and will probably make a commitment towards helping you. As shown on the sample, you may find it useful to jot down a specific reminder beside this prompter.

''Job information'' reminds you to briefly tell your contact what kind of job you're looking for and what your qualifications are. Your best way of doing this is simply to read aloud your own information card. It's exact, brief, and to the point.

As has been said, the remaining prompters relate to questions you should ask the contact. Since there isn't room on the card for the complete questions, you have to use the prompters as starting points and make up the actual questions in your own words.

Take, for example, the prompter ''Being promoted?'' This really means ''Do you know of anyone who is being promoted?'' That's the question you need to ask your contact. To understand the remaining questions, just expand on all of the other prompters in the same way.

Perhaps you may not immediately see the point of *asking* questions about other people's promotions. ''Nice for them but where do I come in?'' you might wonder. Well, as the next chapter will explain in detail, the other people's former positions will now have to be filled and those vacancies can become job leads for you. That's why it's so important to find out about any job changes that may be occurring.

You will notice that the same technique discussed earlier in this chapter has been used here again for these prompters. You don't ask your contact just the one large, general question, ''Do you know of any jobs?'' The person would probably reply ''No,'' to that!

Instead, you break your job question down into the many specific questions suggested by the prompters. You give your contact lots of *definite* things to think about. This makes it much more likely that the person will be able to come up with some positive answers for you.

Remember to use a new contact card for every person you call. Use the back of each card to record important points about every conversation. Don't rely on your memory to hold all this information. Doing so doesn't always work out well and it's not good business practice.

Now let's go back to the "Return call" line on the card. Probably the most important part of using contact cards is filling in the "Return call" lines and then calling back on schedule. After all, you're asking your contacts to check with other people about any job openings in your field. You need to *hear about* the results of their efforts.

Don't accept "I'll call you back," from your contacts, or your number of responses will be very small. *You must take command* and arrange for a time to call your contacts yourself. A good "rule of thumb" is to wait four days and then call back. Give each contact the choice of a time to be called back. Then write down every date and time arranged, using the "Return call" line on each contact card.

If you don't call back on schedule, you will lose! Some contact might have news about a great job waiting for you! In your appointment/date book, write down the details of every call you've arranged. As an added safeguard, it's also suggested that you keep your contact cards in a calendar file to help ensure that you return all your calls to your contacts at the times and dates you've promised. That way, you won't lose out on any good job opportunities that might come along.

Information Cards for Your Contacts

Here's where the information card you prepared in the last chapter really comes into play! As already mentioned, you should read your information card to your contacts when you first call them. Then, if at all possible, you should follow up all positive phone conversations by giving information cards to every committed first-line contact. Remember, if you can get a supply of these cards into the hands of each first-line person who's promised to help you, your "mini résumé" will soon be circulating all over town!

As you remember from the *Circle of Contacts* diagram, networking quickly expands from one contact into dozens. These networking contacts are really sales representatives marketing a product—you! They need good resource materials to describe that product. Therefore, make sure your contacts are well supplied with information cards so that they can give solid facts about you to all potential employers.

Your Supply of Contact Cards

As mentioned earlier, a supply of blank contact cards is now provided here for your use. You may photocopy these cards. Or, if you prefer, you may make your own contact cards, based on these models, using lined index cards. With these cards, you will be able to set up your own contacts file and let the "networking secret" start working for you.

Contact Card

Name: _____ Phone: _____

First call: _____ Return call: _____

- ☐ Reason for call
- ☐ About contact
- ☐ Job information
- ☐ Being promoted?
- ☐ Being transferred?
- ☐ Retiring/leaving?
- ☐ Starting new job?
- ☐ Getting new boss?

- ☐ Know any owners?
- ☐ Know of new firms?
- ☐ Companies growing?
- ☐ Companies hiring?
- ☐ Ask relatives?
- ☐ Ask acquaintances?
- ☐ Ask supervisor?
- ☐ Ask personnel?

Contact Card

Name: _____ Phone: _____

First call: _____ Return call: _____

- ☐ Reason for call
- ☐ About contact
- ☐ Job information
- ☐ Being promoted?
- ☐ Being transferred?
- ☐ Retiring/leaving?
- ☐ Starting new job?
- ☐ Getting new boss?

- ☐ Know any owners?
- ☐ Know of new firms?
- ☐ Companies growing?
- ☐ Companies hiring?
- ☐ Ask relatives?
- ☐ Ask acquaintances?
- ☐ Ask supervisor?
- ☐ Ask personnel?

Contact Card

Name: _____ Phone: _____

First call: _____ Return call: _____

- ☐ Reason for call
- ☐ About contact
- ☐ Job information
- ☐ Being promoted?
- ☐ Being transferred?
- ☐ Retiring/leaving?
- ☐ Starting new job?
- ☐ Getting new boss?

- ☐ Know any owners?
- ☐ Know of new firms?
- ☐ Companies growing?
- ☐ Companies hiring?
- ☐ Ask relatives?
- ☐ Ask acquaintances?
- ☐ Ask supervisor?
- ☐ Ask personnel?

Contact Card

Name: _____ Phone: _____

First call: _____ Return call: _____

- ☐ Reason for call
- ☐ About contact
- ☐ Job information
- ☐ Being promoted?
- ☐ Being transferred?
- ☐ Retiring/leaving?
- ☐ Starting new job?
- ☐ Getting new boss?

- ☐ Know any owners?
- ☐ Know of new firms?
- ☐ Companies growing?
- ☐ Companies hiring?
- ☐ Ask relatives?
- ☐ Ask acquaintances?
- ☐ Ask supervisor?
- ☐ Ask personnel?

5
Discovering Job Leads

5 Discovering Job Leads

Your Job Leads File

By this stage, your job search project is really beginning to get under way! Soon, your network of contacts will be providing you with job leads. You'll also be discovering leads for yourself, using the sources discussed in this chapter.

Writing this job lead information on pieces of scrap paper would be disastrous. Just imagine how many loose scraps of paper you would acquire in your search and how easily these scraps might become lost.

To avoid this problem and safely keep track of all your different leads, you need to set up a job leads file for yourself. Another special index card—the job lead card—has been designed for this purpose. You should make up one of these cards every time you or your contacts discover a lead for a job.

As you process each job lead, fill in the appropriate lines on the card. Fill in the last section, "Results/notes," once you've had an interview. Keep each card in an indexed file box for reference.

A sample card has been completed for you below. Blank job lead cards have also been provided for your personal use. You may either photocopy these cards or make up your own, using lined index cards.

Job Lead Card—Sample

Lead source: *Aunt Joyce Nguyen*   Date rec'd: *June 27*

Position: *Posting clerk -- assistant supervisor trainee*

Company name: *Cameron + Burns, Inc.*   Phone: *435 - 8595*

Company address: *35 3rd Ave., N.W., Calgary, Alta. T2N 0J2*

Interview date: *July 5*   Time: *2:30*

Interview location: *35 3rd Ave., New York, N.Y. 10003*

Name of interviewer: *David Cameron*   Title: *Partner*

Results/notes: *Pleasant people; clean, well-run office; to see Ms. Burns, July 12, 11:15, Suite 2 for 2nd interview; take reference from Len Bargowski*

Job Lead Card

Lead source: _____ Date rec'd: _____

Position: _____

Company name: _____ Phone: _____

Company address: _____

Interview date: _____ Time: _____

Interview location: _____

Name of interviewer: _____ Title: _____

Results/notes: _____

_____

_____

Job Lead Card

Lead source: _____ Date rec'd: _____

Position: _____

Company name: _____ Phone: _____

Company address: _____

Interview date: _____ Time: _____

Interview location: _____

Name of interviewer: _____ Title: _____

Results/notes: _____

_____

_____

Job Lead Card

Lead source: _____ Date rec'd: _____

Position: _____

Company name: _____ Phone: _____

Company address: _____

Interview date: _____ Time: _____

Interview location: _____

Name of interviewer: _____ Title: _____

Results/notes: _____

_____

_____

Job Lead Card

Lead source: _____ Date rec'd: _____

Position: _____

Company name: _____ Phone: _____

Company address: _____

Interview date: _____ Time: _____

Interview location: _____

Name of interviewer: _____ Title: _____

Results/notes: _____

_____

_____

Visible Job Markets

Jobs appear in two areas—visible and hidden markets. Advertised
positions and publicized vacancies are the "visible" job market.

Newspaper Advertisements

"Help wanted," and "Careers" sections of your local newspapers
are the best visible markets. When using these sources, you must
carefully read *every* ad, *every* day. Many employers only advertise once.
Their reason for when and where to advertise is sometimes difficult
to understand.

When reading advertisements, you must look *beyond* what is written.
Most qualifications are stated as minimum; however, if the word
"preferred" is used, this means the employer will consider less *or* the
combination of skills and experience. Some employers use advertising to
assist in weeding out unsuitable applicants. These employers place carefully
worded instructions in their ads and reject applicants who cannot follow
these instructions. Have you ever encountered this situation?

Job Agencies

Personnel and employment agencies provide another visible market.

Private personnel agencies have lists of paying clients with immediate
job openings to be filled. You must register with the agency and be
ready to go for an interview on short notice. Agencies take job orders
from clients for specific positions, so be prepared to identify a "specific
interest" area and prove your skills by means of various tests. You
must understand, however, that if the agency does not have a current
order from a client requiring your particular skills, you may remain in the
files for some time with no guarantee of finding a job in the near
future. Find out how often each agency updates its files and check back
regularly to keep your application "current."

Government employment centers offer a *free* service to employers
who want to fill positions within their companies. Again, you must
register with your district office and be prepared to identify your skill
area.

Hidden Job Markets

Approximately 80 per cent of jobs are filled without government or
private-agency assistance or without being advertised. These jobs come
from the hidden market.

To use this market, you must look for information about "holes" that need to be filled in various organizations. Clues to locating this information appear in newspapers, magazines, and industry trade journals.

Many occupations support their own particular trade journals. These trade journals give you an indication of specific markets and show you where to find expansion and movement within the industry. Your local library can supply you with a list of trade journal titles and tell you how to go about ordering your own copies of these publications.

The library is also a good place to consult trade directories and out-of-town newspapers and telephone directories. State and national trade directories give detailed information on individual companies. Telephone ''Yellow Pages'' give names, addresses, and additional details on companies in specific trades or industries. So if you're willing to move, check out these out-of-town sources for jobs.

Finding the Clues

When you've done your research at the library and purchased a supply of useful publications, you're ready to get down to business. Armed with a pen or felt marker, go through all your newspapers, magazines, and trade journals from cover to cover. As you read, *cross out* and discard the articles and announcements that don't contain job hints. *Circle* the ones that should be given further consideration or investigation. Remember this is a *hunt* for a job, so be careful not to overlook *any* clues given in these articles.

Listed below are some ''avenues'' or ''holes'' that the majority of job seekers *never* consider. Clues to them can be found in your local newspapers, trade journals, or news magazines. As you will realize when you start reading about these ''avenues,'' you already have your network of contacts asking questions about ''holes'' like these on your behalf. So, with your own researches and the inquiries of your contacts, you have an excellent chance of discovering job leads from these sources.

Promotion Announcements

When employees are promoted within their companies, their old jobs are usually filled by other persons. If a promotion is at a senior level, the person filling the ''hole'' will probably be another employee of the same company. However, this does not always happen. Even if the process *is* internal, somewhere in the organization a vacant position will probably go to the outside for filling. If you want to get into the company, contact them to see at what level they are recruiting. It may be a position just for you.

Transfers and Retirements

Like promotions, transfers and retirements create vacancies that have a high chance of being filled. Inquire to see what the job opportunities are within the company.

Company Expansion

When companies expand their services or product lines, they usually require additional staff to meet their new commitments. Don't wait to apply until a company begins to advertise. You will then just be grouped in with all the other applicants! If your skills go along with the service or product being manufactured, *make the first move and contact the company.*

Company Relocation

When you hear of companies moving or relocating to another area, contact them to offer your services for positions that may become available. For many reasons, employees often do not want to relocate with their companies. Moving an entire family from one city to another causes more disruption than some people are willing to take. Even moves across the city may be an inconvenience that will cause some employees to resign. Again, don't wait to be asked. *Make the first move.*

Announcements and Awards

New product announcements and notices of contract awards mean more work and the possibility of hiring additional staff or staff with different skills. *Take the initiative and make the contact.*

Company Mergers and Takeovers

When mergers and takeovers take place, new owners usually reassess the present employees and lay off employees with duplicate jobs or skills not required by the new organization. To discover what skills a company is now looking for, you may wish to let the new owners know what you have done, what you can do, and where you wish to work. Remember, nothing ventured, nothing gained!

Career Ads for Executive Officers

The old saying, ''The new broom sweeps clean,'' means that new managers and executives are always on the alert to remove nonproductive employees and replace them with dependable people. If you are known to a new manager who is taking over, you may have an excellent chance of being hired.

6

Deleting Job Leads

6 Deleting Job Leads

As you follow through on your job leads, there are many factors to consider before accepting a position. Some jobs may *sound* good but they may have conditions that will prevent you from feeling comfortable in many ways, once you've started work. So to avoid getting trapped in the wrong employment, it's important to be very clear on what you actually *expect* from your ideal job. As a first step towards this, you need to be able to define your general expectations as an employee.

Employee Expectations

Everyone has certain expectations of others; however, most people's expectations remain undefined, unspoken, and unwritten. People in uncomfortable situations often have strong, general feelings of dissatisfaction without being able to pinpoint or express what's wrong. This particular communication gap is the root of many problems.

Difficulties grow and fester when expectations are not defined and brought to the surface as soon as they are formed. Soon emotions become involved; tempers rise to the boiling point; facts are distorted; and what began as a minor problem may have a lasting effect on the parties concerned.

Back in Chapter 2, you filled in a chart listing the expectations of the employer. Well, in the business world expectations exist on both sides—employer *and* employees. To see things now from an employee's side—your side—fill in the *Chart of Employee Expectations* given on page 67.

In this chart, list the general conditions you will expect to find in your job. You may possibly want to include conditions such as being paid regularly, being respected, having job security, and being fairly treated. When you've come up with a list of ten conditions, number them in their priority order of personal importance to you.

A sample *Chart of Employee Expectations* has been filled in for you on page 69. Do you agree with the conditions listed in this example and with their priority ordering? Would you expect any of the same things yourself?

Chart of Employer Expectations

Quality Expected   **Priority Order**

1. _____

2. _____

3. _____

4. _____

5. _____

6. _____

7. _____

8. _____

9. _____

10. _____

It's interesting to note that the majority of people—whether young or old, educated or uneducated, male or female—have similar expectations regarding their jobs. To test this for yourself, try making some photocopies of the *Chart of Employee Expectations* before filling in this chart for yourself. Ask your relatives and friends to fill in these blank copies. Then compare their expectations with your own. You'll find this an interesting experiment!

Chart of Employee Expectations—Sample

	Condition Expected	Priority Order
1.	Get paid	1
2.	Be treated fairly	2
3.	Have nice work area	9
4.	Have good boss	4
5.	Have good benefits plan	8
6.	Have good vacation plan	10
7.	Receive training	6
8.	Be respected	5
9.	Have job security	3
10.	Have friendly co-workers	7

Conditions To Avoid

Once you know generally what you expect as an employee, you also need to identify the specific working conditions you do *not* want to find in your ideal job. It's important to go through the list of questions given below and decide on your own personal answers to each of them. Then, for every job lead you receive, check whether any conditions in that particular job are contrary to the answers you've given. If some conditions aren't right, then delete the lead. Failure to do so could mean ending up in the wrong job.

What Environment Do I Find Unsuitable?

It's *physical* working conditions that are important here. If you have allergies, for example, then a job in a dusty work area could aggravate those allergies and cause you discomfort. More importantly, this health problem could cause you to have time away from work. Your employer might look upon this as unsatisfactory behavior and terminate your employment.

Where Do I Not Wish To Live?

Everything from climate to personal preferences may affect whether or not you wish to live in certain parts of the country. The South may be too hot for you. The North may be too cold. The West Coast may be too wet.

Another factor to consider is distance from home. Working thousands of miles from home makes returning on a regular basis difficult. For one thing, it's too costly! If you have friends or relatives who are ailing, you may not wish to be far away from them during their illness. *You* must make this decision.

What Jobs or Industries Offend My Beliefs?

People don't always feel personally concerned about the industry they work in or about the services or products supplied by their companies. For reasons of principle, however, people sometimes may not want to work in certain areas.

Are there moral issues about which you feel strongly? If so, find out whether these issues will be involved in your employment. Remember, to be a good employee you must work in surroundings that do not conflict with your inner beliefs. Otherwise, the conflict will be reflected in your performance.

What Personality Traits Do I Find Unpleasant?

If you know something in advance about the personalities of the people with whom you will be working, this knowledge may influence you against taking the job. If you dislike people who are rude, overbearing, and bossy, then why take a job where you will have to work with them? Just imagine what you will feel like at the end of each day spent with these people!

Am I Willing To Work Overtime?

If the employer requires overtime on a regular basis—and your personal commitments conflict with this—be fair to both the employer and yourself and look for work in another company.

Am I Willing To Work Nights and Weekends?

Essential departments such as police, fire, health emergency, and public transportation *must* provide around-the-clock service. Because of product demand or restricted physical areas, many businesses must also operate more than five days per week and during hours outside the regular daytime shifts. As with the previous section, if you cannot or will not work under these conditions, then don't make the mistake of accepting such a job.

Am I Willing To Relocate or Travel?

Suppose you tell an employer at an interview that you will accept being transferred after training or after a suitable period of time with the company. If you later refuse a transfer when it's offered, what do you think will happen? The employer will probably terminate your employment! The employer is hiring people who will work under the conditions required for the successful operation of the company. If, for whatever reason, you cannot leave your present city or be away from home on a regular basis, don't promise to do so during an interview. Instead, look for a different job.

Salary Requirements

In this whole process of analysing your job leads and deleting the ones which are unsuitable, *salary offered* is the most important point for you to consider.

Taking a job that is under your minimum salary requirements may cause two problems. Firstly, your search for a job with a higher salary figure will continue. You may quit your job for another one offering just a few dollars more. Then you'll wait for another higher-priced job to come along and jump again.

Doing this will give a ''job-hopping'' appearance to your résumé.

Most employers will assume you will only stay with them for a short time until another more suitable job comes along. Since employers know the cost of training and rehiring, they will probably pass you by and look for a more stable person.

Moreover, if you've taken a job that doesn't pay you enough money, you may try to make up your income shortage with a second job. The long hours involved in having two jobs will probably make you exhausted, causing problems to both your performance and your work record. When you're tired, you make mistakes. Furthermore, you will be tempted to call in sick, to one job or the other, when your system cannot find the energy required for so much work. In the end, you may lose *both* jobs and have a work record showing "termination for unsatisfactory behavior."

To avoid all these problems, it's important to have a realistic idea of the amount of salary you will need. The *Monthly Personal Budget Chart* on page 73 will help you to achieve this.

Complete this chart considering all the expenses you might have in any one month of the year. Make adjustments for annual payments such as home or auto insurance and other large expenses that come only once a year—vacations, for example. Then hold out for a job that will provide you with enough *take-home* pay to cover the amount you've listed for "Total Expenses." Remember that employers quote in *gross* amounts of salary. So, for each job you're offered, decide whether the *net* pay, after deductions, will cover your expenses. If it won't, don't take the job!

Monthly Personal Budget Chart

Item	Amount

Housing:

- Rent or mortage payments (include taxes) $ _____
- Electricity   _____
- Heat   _____
- Maintenance and property repairs   _____
- Cable television   _____
- Telephone   _____
- Insurance   _____

Transportation:

- Public transportation   _____
- Automobile:
  - Gas and oil   _____
  - Insurance and license yearly divided by pays per year   _____
  - Repairs (estimated—include service)   _____

Living Expenses:

- Groceries (include lunch expenses at work, soft drinks, etc.)   _____
- Clothes   _____
- Newspapers, magazines, books   _____
- Cigarettes, alcohol   _____
- Entertainment (include any baby-sitting expenses)   _____
- Spending money and donations   _____

Loans/Savings:

- Savings (bank account, bonds, etc.)   _____
- Car payments   _____
- Furniture payments   _____
- Loans from relatives and friends   _____
- Charge accounts, credit cards, legal expenses   _____

Other:

- Dentists, prescriptions   _____
- Vacations, gifts, unforeseen expenses   _____

Total Expenses: $ _____

7
Telephoning Employers

7 Telephoning Employers

Telephone Techniques

Using the telephone successfully is a very important part of your job search program. A good phone call can be the means of turning a job lead into a job offer! To achieve this, however, you must know how to use effective telephone techniques.

Points for Successful Phone Calls

A phone call to an employer should be brief but it should state *who* you are, *why* you're calling, *what* you can offer, and *when* you can come in for an interview. Let's take a quick look at each of these points.

Introducing Yourself

In a strong but not overbearing voice, introduce yourself at the start of the conversation. Everyone is cautious about talking to nameless callers! Begin something like this: ''Hello, Ms. Sawdon, my name is Mark Paulin.''

Explaining Your Call

Tell the person you've reached why you're calling. Don't prolong your explanation because the person you're talking to may be very busy. You might say, for example: ''I'm interested in a position with your company as a receptionist,'' or ''I'm interested in the open position of receptionist.''

Offering Your Talents

What you have to offer *must* be the ''hook of interest'' that will make the person you are calling want to meet you face to face. *The statement you make here is the most important part of your call*. It must contain:

- What you have done
- What you can do
- What you want to do for this company

Before making the call, review your career capsule and career goal since they contain most of the information you should give.

Obtaining an Interview

The reason for the telephone call is to get an interview—*so ask for one!* Most inexperienced people give a choice between something and "nothing." They might ask, for example: "Will Monday at 11:30 be all right?" This question is too risky and may end up with the answer, "No." *Never leave that option open.*

Successful salespeople know how to give a "choice" to their customers. Do the same here. In asking for an interview, give a choice between two days or times. Say, for example: "I'm available both Monday and Tuesday." Or ask: "Would Monday morning at 9:00 be convenient for you or would Tuesday afternoon at 4:00 suit you better?" If both times are inconvenient, then negotiate a time acceptable to both of you.

The Need for Counter Responses

The points outlined above show the ideal flow of a telephone conversation, from giving your name down to confirming an interview time. However, it's unrealistic to expect every phone call to go smoothly! You may often be met with the word "no" during your conversations. It's a good plan to consider the areas where "no's" may arise during a phone call and prepare short but effective counter responses. Let's look at some of these areas now.

Responding to "Position Filled"

How would you respond if you were the caller in the following example?

- **Caller:** 'Mr. Borowski, my name is Dan Cheung. I'm calling you regarding the advertised position of assistant buyer."
- **Employer:** I'm sorry, Mr. Cheung, but we hired someone for that position yesterday."

The majority of people—90 to 95 per cent—would respond with a comment something like this:

- **Caller:** "Oh! I see. Well thank you for speaking with me. Good-bye."

This answer doesn't follow through on the employment prospects *still remaining* in this job lead!

When an employer says, "The position has been filled," consider the following possibilities:

- The new person may not show up to work on the first day. It happens!
- The new person may not be what the interviewer expected and may be dismissed. It happens!
- The new person may not be happy with the job and may resign. It happens!

- Another position may become vacant in the company. It happens!

Therefore, a wise caller will answer with a counter response that keeps the door open to these possibilities.

Consider the following counter responses to Mr. Borowski's statement that the assistant buyer position has been filled:

- **Caller:** ''Mr. Borowski, I understand that it is important to hire good people as soon as possible. However, since I have all the qualifications asked for in your advertisement—plus others— would you please consider meeting with me next week? That way, you'll have a qualified back-up person available in case you need a second assistant, or in case something unforeseen happens with the new employee. Would Wednesday after lunch be all right or would early Thursday morning be better?''

OR

- **Caller:** ''I'm sorry I didn't reach you sooner, Mr. Borowski, as I feel my education and experience in this area would have been interesting to you. Mr. Borowski, even though you have given the job to someone else, I would still like to meet with you next week to share some ideas I have on what I could do for your company. Is next Tuesday afternoon suitable for you or would Friday morning at 9:00 be better?''

OR

- **Caller:** ''I'm really sorry to hear that, Mr. Borowski. I've looked into your company and would certainly appreciate an opportunity to work for a firm like yours. Mr. Borowski, if you would give me a few minutes of your day, I'd like to introduce myself in person to explain my career goal. Could I meet with you early next Monday, or would Tuesday be better?''

Always remember that the objective of your call is *to get an appointment!* Let's look at one more example, this time using a slightly different statement by Mr. Borowski:

- **Employer:** ''I'm sorry, Mr. Cheung, but we promoted a present company office employee into this position yesterday.''
- **Caller:** ''Mr. Borowski, I'm happy to know that your company has the policy of promoting from within. Would you consider me for the other employee's former position? I do have experience in office work and office supervision, as well as in sales and buying. Could I meet with you on Thursday afternoon, or would you prefer Friday morning?''

Responding to Other Refusals

Role playing can be a very helpful way of learning how to make effective counter responses. With this in mind, act out some phone call situations for yourself, taking both the employer's role and the caller's role. Come up with as many different refusals and counter responses as possible. Then try them out on your family and friends to get their reactions. To help you get started on role playing, read through the further example situations given below:

- **Employer:** "I don't have the time to see you right now."
- **Caller:** "From the information I have on your company, Ms. Hamza, I know that you're very busy and I certainly understand what you're saying. However, if we could meet next week on Tuesday at 8:00 or Wednesday at 5:00, I know you'd find my background in marketing an advantage in helping with your heavy workload."

- **Employer:** "All our hiring is done by the head office."
- **Caller:** "I understand, Mr. Donnetti. Would you suggest that I write or call the head office directly for more information on positions within your company?"
- **Employer:** "Yes, that would be the best idea."
- **Caller:** "Well, in that case, Mr. Donnetti, would you please give me the name and position of the person I should contact? Would you also permit me to refer to our conversation?"

- **Employer:** "We're not accepting any more applications."
- **Caller:** "I understand that your company must place a deadline on accepting applications, Ms. Querido. However, I know my past experience and knowledge in your industry would certainly be an asset to your company. Even though you're not accepting further applications for the advertised position, may I please meet with you briefly, on Monday at 11:00 or Wednesday at 3:00 to introduce myself personally?"

- **Employer:** "No! I'm not interested!"
- **Caller:** "Perhaps I could contact you at a later date, Mr. Grunwald, to see if the situation has changed in your company. In the meantime, would you permit me to send you my résumé with a covering letter to explain further my interest in your firm?"

In all of the above situations, the point to remember always remains the same. *Be polite but be persistent!*

Handling Telephone Rejections

Despite all the role playing and preparing you've done, it's understandable that you may find it upsetting to experience a "rough" phone call. When you feel this way, remember a statement that was made earlier in this chapter: "It's unrealistic to expect every phone call to go smoothly!"

Rejections do happen—and sometimes too frequently. Not all employers are polite and helpful when they are called. However, there could be numerous reasons for an abrupt response or annoyed tone of voice. Perhaps you've just reached a person at a bad time. Suggest calling back later.

Sometimes, though, a "no" is followed by the crashing sound of an employer banging down the phone immediately. It does happen! To help soothe your feelings and get you back on the track in such a situation, ask yourself this question: "Would I even *want* to work for someone who could be that rude and curt to a stranger?" Of course you wouldn't! So it's a good thing you identified this person's business characteristics now, before you went any further with that company. Just delete the lead and keep on smiling. There are lots of better jobs available!

Lead Replacement

As you know, one of the most important parts of your job search program is having a plentiful supply of job leads. When you use a lead, try and replace it immediately—*never* let your leads run out.

Your phone calls to employers are actually one of your best sources for further job leads. Sometimes during a phone conversation with an employer, it will become evident that the possibility of obtaining an interview at this time is not going to materialize. In that case, try to obtain another job lead from the person with whom you are speaking.

You have just spent time telling this person what you have done, what your strengths are, and where you want to go over the next few years. Since there are no openings or opportunities in this person's company, *ask* what other companies might be interested in the experience and skills you've outlined. Right now, this may seem like the hardest thing imaginable to do; but after you've tried it a few times it will become easier. You'll be surprised at the number of people who will offer suggestions and leads for you to follow up.

Here is an example of how to word your request: "Ms. Arroyo, it's unfortunate that we cannot meet at this time. However, since you're now familiar with my background and career goal, could you suggest an employer in your industry who might be interested in someone with my qualifications?" If Ms. Arroyo does give you a lead, ask whether you may use her name when you call that employer. Being able to give a name always makes it easier to get through.

To sum it all up, *always* try to replace *every* lead that doesn't work out. If your leads are running low, you're not asking for more leads. It's as simple as that!

8
Answering Advertisements

8 Answering Advertisements

Letter Techniques

In Chapter 3, the subject of writing covering letters was discussed in detail. Basically, most of the same points mentioned there also apply to letters written in answer to advertisements. There's one difference that should be noted, however. When you're answering a newspaper ad, it's sometimes not possible to address your letter to a specific individual. In that case, the form of address "Dear Sir or Madam" is acceptable.

On the following pages, you'll find several examples of newspaper ads accompanied by application letters responding to them. As you read these letters, notice how the wording used in them "hooks" the reader's interest. As with all covering letters and all phone calls to employers, the basic purpose of these application letters is *to obtain an interview*. Study the means employed in these letters to achieve this purpose. Then use the same techniques in your own application letters.

RECEPTIONIST/CLERK

The person we are looking for will cover a wide variety of duties in this downtown office. Computer experience is a definite asset. We are only interested in talking to people who possess the following qualifications—accurate keyboarding speed of 45 wpm; good grooming; excellent telephone voice and manner; good memory; minimum of one year's general office experience.

We offer an excellent starting salary, a complete benefit package, and opportunities to advance to other locations of the company. Please reply no later than the 15th of this month, sending your résumé, the name of one reference, and your salary expectations to: Ms. Patricia Cameron, Manager, Northern Relocaters Inc. 1045 Harvey Avenue, Tacoma, WA 98404.

573 Poplar Road
Tacoma, WA 98421
January 5, 19—

Ms. Patricia Cameron, Manager
Northern Relocaters Inc.
1045 Harvey Avenue
Tacoma, WA 98404

Dear Ms. Cameron:

I am applying for the position of Receptionist/Clerk that was advertised in today's *Tacoma Daily Courier.*

Since you have offered student work experience in your company, your firm is well known to many students at Whitney Township High School, my old high school. In fact, I was one of the students who worked for two weeks in your office. At Whitney, I took regular and computer keyboarding with a speed of 55 wpm. During my work experience with Northern Relocaters, I worked for several half days entering data into your computer system.

Currently, I am working for the Shuster Insurance Agency as an office clerk handling most of the general office duties. As the office is located in the Century Plaza, I must be professionally dressed at all times. Although I enjoy my job with Shusters, it is a small family-owned business with no advancement opportunities. This is my reason for replying to your advertisement.

My salary expectations would be $800 to $1000 per month. Mrs. Cynthia Wrought has agreed to provide me with a reference. Mrs. Wrought is a neighbor for whom I have done baby-sitting over the last four years. Her phone number is 555-3876. Thank you very much for considering this application. I am looking forward to hearing from you in the near future. I can be reached at 555-7066 or 555-2047.

Yours truly,

Tammy Unger

Tammy Unger

Enc: Résumé

SECURITY OFFICER

We are accepting applications for the position of Security Officer to work out of our downtown office. Extensive training will be provided.

Applicants must be well-groomed, physically fit, have good communication skills, own a car, and have a good driving record. In addition, applicants must be bondable. Previous experience would be an asset.

Please address your reply to: Data Security Services, 5237 Young Street, Wilmington, DE 19808.

5679 Fenwick Street
Wilmington, DE 19802
September 12, 19—

Data Security Services
5237 Young Street
Wilmington, DE 19808

Dear Sir or Madam:

Would you please accept this letter of application for the position of Security Officer in your downtown office, as advertised in today's *Herald?*

I do possess the basic requirements stated in your advertisement. I have never had any accidents or traffic tickets since I received my driver's license. While in school, I assisted on several occasions to control visitors during concerts and sports events. I also worked in the information booth helping new students and parents find their way around the school.

I am willing to work all shifts including Saturdays, Sundays, and holidays. I am also willing to move as I know that Data Security Services has several locations in Delaware as well as offices in three other states. Currently, I own a four-door Chevrolet which I purchased new only two years ago.

I will contact your office at the end of this week to arrange an interview time convenient to your schedule.

Yours truly,

Leslie Chan

Leslie Chan

Enc: Résumé

518 Willow Street, Apt. 3C
Saskatoon, Saskatchewan
S7J 0C9
March 26, 19--

Personnel Officer
Grey Medical Center
P.O. Box 30
Grey, ND 58561

Dear Sir or Madam:

I read your advertisement in the *Saskatoon Star Phoenix* on Saturday, March 25, and request that you consider my application for the position of Registered Nurse.

I have a degree in Nursing from the University of Ottawa. I have worked for three years at the Ottawa Civic Hospital in the intensive care unit, and am presently employed with the City Hospital in Saskatoon.

My home is Fargo, North Dakota. When I was visiting home last month, I had occasion to make a call at your medical center. The professionalism shown by your admittance and nursing staff was impressive. Your center has the kind of atmosphere in which I would like to work. I have been considering returning to the United States, and now this timely career opportunity you have at the center would fit into my plans very well.

My résumé details my nursing education and experience. I have always had a genuine interest in health care since I was a youngster, and I was a hospital volunteer throughout most of my high school years. This background, plus my very high marks, won me a scholarship to the Faculty of Nursing at the University of Ottawa. I feel that with my education, enthusiasm, work experience in this field of nursing, and familiarity with your organization, I would be a definite asset to your medical center.

At the end of this week, I will be visiting Fargo for about ten days. I will contact you while I am there to make arrangements for an interview where I can expand on my background and how it can be of assistance to the Grey Medical Center.

Yours truly,

Jerry Wolanska

Jerry Wolanska

Enc: Résumé

MANAGEMENT TRAINEE

On August 15, we will be starting a management-trainee program for six persons having the qualifications we feel our management candidates should possess. We require high school graduation (proof needed), good grooming, physical fitness, excellent oral and written communication skills, proven leadership skills, and excellent mechanical aptitude.

If you are interested and possess these requirements, please send your résumé to our personnel department at: First-Lite Mechanical Warehouse Inc., 37 Division Street, Little Rock, AR 72209.

27 Purdy Place, Apt. 509
Little Rock, AR 72204
July 28, 19—

Personnel Department
First-Lite Mechanical Warehouse Inc.
Little Rock, AR 72209

Dear Sir or Madam:

Would you please accept this letter and attached résumé for consideration in regard to the position of Management Trainee advertised in today's *Standard*?

I have received my High School Diploma and have also graduated with a Certificate in Mechanical Technology from Cooper College near Bentonville. Last year, a representative from your company came to Cooper and explained in detail the training program for which you are now recruiting. I am very eager to be considered for this program as I know other people who have had this training and are now assistant managers within your organization.

I do possess all of the qualifications listed in your advertisement. When I was in high school, I took a special course in supervisory and management skills for students, like myself, who were on the student council. This course helped me to develop leadership skills, as did my position as captain of the school softball team.

Since this opportunity is very important to me and my career goal, I will call you next week to answer any of your questions and to arrange a meeting that will suit your convenience.

Yours truly,

Daria Rossetti

Daria Rossetti

Enc: Résumé

INSURANCE CLERK

We have an immediate opening for a person capable of handling customer inquiries and personal insurance claims. Applicants must have a minimum of 35 wpm keyboarding skills, be well-groomed, and be willing to work every Saturday.

If you have the qualifications we require, please send your résumé to Mr. Albert Side, Side Insurance Brokers, 39 Elizabeth Avenue, Erie, Pa 16505.

15 Pennywell Road, Apt. 2B
Erie, PA 16507
November 8, 19—

Mr. Albert Side
Side Insurance Brokers
39 Elizabeth Avenue
Erie, PA 16505

Dear Mr. Side:

I read with interest your advertisement in today's *Daily News* for an Insurance Clerk.

Before I moved to Erie this fall, my previous work experience was at the Main Insurance Bureau in Corner Brook. Although I was employed there on a part-time basis while attending school, I did work at the Bureau for three years on Saturdays and Friday evenings. During this time, I was given assignments in various areas in the office including reception, steno services (my keyboarding speed is 50 wpm), new policy administration, and claims investigation.

I feel that my background in insurance, both personal and property, would be an asset to your company. I will call you at the end of this week to arrange an interview at which time I can show you a letter of reference from the manager of the Main Insurance Bureau.

Yours truly,

Robin Mayberry

Robin Mayberry

Enc: Résumé

PARTS BUYER

If you have experience working with truck, and trailer parts, we have a great career opportunity for you with a large international trucking firm. Our client is looking for a self-motivated person experienced in locating and purchasing truck and trailer parts, and in writing service orders. Familiarity with computer-assisted inventory systems would be an asset.

This a a full-time position with a salary range of $22,000 to $28,000 annually. If you possess good communication and people skills and are eager to work hard for your future, we would like to talk with you. Please apply to: Recruitment Canada, 360 Main Street, Suite 1670, Jakson, MS 39213.

390 Lakeshore Road
Jackson, MS 39212
May 20, 19—

Recruitment Systems
360 Main Street, Suite 1670
Jackson, MS 39213

Dear Sir or Madam:

I am an experienced truck and trailer parts buyer and wish to be considered for the position that was advertised in the *Free Press* on Saturday, May 18.

As stated in my attached résumé, I have worked for two years in the parts and purchasing department of a major trucking firm. My current position with this company is that of special purchasing agent for parts and supplies for trucks and truck trailers. I specialize in those parts which are difficult to find and usually needed on short notice. Our current inventory and available suppliers for these parts are computerized on a software program I developed this year.

I know that your client will recognize my current employer and understand the situation our company is in because of the impending takeover by a larger firm. This is my reason for seeking to make a change at this time.

Some of my strengths are being hard-working, self-motivated, and easy to work with. I consider my people skills to be very good as I supervise two office assistants and am very successful in dealing with these staff members and also with suppliers. If you wish to see my past-performance evaluations from my current employer, I will be pleased to bring them to the interview.

You can contact me at work (555-8625) or leave a message on my answering machine at home (555-4197). I believe strongly that my current responsibilities give me the potential to be a definite asset to your client.

Yours truly,

Maurice LeRoux

Enc: Résumé

9

Winning at Interviews

9 Winning at Interviews

Interview Guidelines

There are dozens of "dos" and "don'ts" involved in handling interviews effectively. Experience is the best teacher of what should be done and said during an interview. However, the guidelines provided here should also prove very useful in helping you to come out a "winner" from those all-important interviews.

What Not To Do

The "don'ts" listed below represent *negative* factors that should be eliminated from your interviews. Otherwise, these factors may eliminate *you* from the competition! Employers realize that these negative factors pinpoint areas where extra training will be needed to change an applicant's bad habits. Naturally, employers prefer to hire those applicants who show the fewest signs of negative behavior. Such people make an employer's job of training much easier. So here are the negative factors to avoid:

- **Don't bring the "kitchen sink":** Bring only the paperwork needed to support the first interview unless you have received specific instructions otherwise, from the interviewer or from the advertisement. Seeing your excess baggage may make the interviewer feel uncomfortable.

- **Don't tell jokes or comment on people in the office:** Not knowing the interviewer's background or social, religious, or political beliefs, you can cause some very uncomfortable feelings by making off-color jokes or comments in an attempt to break the ice in the interview. Keep to safe topics such as the weather or the local sports team.

- **Don't use negative body language:** Negative body language is any action that closes out the interviewer. Crossing your arms or legs, glancing around the room, or sliding down in the chair tells the interviewer that your interest has gone. This may lead to the interviewer losing interest in *you*.

- **Don't smile like a toothpaste commercial:** Although a smile doesn't hurt anyone, it can be overdone. It then becomes a distraction. Distractions of any kind will draw the attention of the interviewer away from what you are saying. When this happens, there is a risk that the interviewer may not hear that *all-important point* you are trying to make.

- **Don't bring other people with you to the interview:** What would you do if the interviewer asked you to stay and start the job immediately? If you have young children, leave them with a baby-sitter. If you have a ride waiting, ask the person to stay in the car. If you have someone along for moral support, listen to your friend's last words of encouragement *before* you enter the interview building. The fact is that some employers may not want to break up you and your ''buddy.'' Therefore, they may offer the job to the next qualified applicant who comes alone. It does happen!

- **Don't be a name-dropper:** What happens if the name you ''drop'' belongs to a person not admired by the interviewer? In fact, if the person whose name you are using to ''influence'' the interviewer is disliked by the interviewer for some reason, you may have lost this job opportunity.

- **Don't limit your time for the interview:** For a multitude of reasons, interviews don't always start on time. Also, interviews can last for fifteen minutes or for two hours. The amount of time all depends on the interviewer's style and on how much interest is caused by your application. If you book interviews too close together, you may have the unfortunate experience of being late or of missing another appointment. A good rule of thumb is to book one interview early in the morning and another one in the afternoon.

- **Don't be late:** Being late may be an indicator of your work habits. Many employers eliminate applicants because of this negative factor.

- **Don't smoke unless you are invited to do so:** More and more employers are introducing smoke-free environments into the work place. *Always* wait to be asked whether you wish to smoke. Even then, it's probably better not to do so unless the interviewer lights a cigarette first.

- **Don't break the silence:** The silent treatment is used by some interviewers to draw out additional information without actually asking the applicant to continue. In many cases, this technique is used when the interviewer is collecting negative information. Applicants don't like the silence and will continue to add information in the subject area being discussed. It's advisable to answer a question to the best of your ability; then *stop talking* and leave it up to the interviewer to continue the conversation.

- **Don't ask questions that show no interest for the job:** Questions such as the color of the office, the length of the coffee breaks, and the size of the work station should not be asked during the first interview. The importance of these questions to you may indicate to the interviewer that you are more concerned with the ''benefits'' of the job than with doing the actual work for the company.

- **Don't be nervous:** This is easy to say, but sometimes difficult to manage. Don't be worried, however, if you *are* nervous. Everyone can be nervous sometimes—even the interviewer. A good interviewer will understand and will put you at ease.

What To Do

Once you know what negative factors to avoid, you must also know what positive factors to emphasize. To help you in this regard, a list of ''dos'' for interview behavior is given a little further below. The first thing you should *do*, however, is make sure you look acceptable. Your personal appearance *must* be suitable for the interview. Since this factor is so important, let's look at it separately, first of all.

Look Acceptable

It's human nature not to want to admit that one has made an error, or that one's judgment has been incorrect. Well, interviewers are only human, after all! Once they've formed an opinion about you, they're not going to want to admit they've been mistaken. For this reason, first impressions are very important at interviews.

The way you look is the first thing an interviewer notices about you. If the interviewer begins by judging your personal appearance to be unacceptable for the job, this will prejudice that interviewer's whole opinion of you. During the rest of the interview, it's very unlikely that the interviewer will put that bad first impression to one side while evaluating your other qualifications and assets. Do you want to take that risk? Of course not! Therefore, it's important to make the best first impression possible. Observing the following points about appearance will help you to achieve this.

One: Always dress as if you were going to start the new job immediately. Your clothing must be co-ordinated in color and style, clean, pressed, and not in need of repairs. Your shoes must be shined and in good condition. Above all, your whole outfit must be suitable for the work you will be doing.

If you have the time, try and find out what the employees of the company wear to work. If you know someone who works there, ask. If you don't, observe employees as they leave work, or visit the company before the interview. Should this not be possible, then consider the outfit you would expect a person to wear to an interview if *you* were the interviewer. Remember that there *is* a difference between business and social dress. Don't make a mistake in this regard or it could cost you the job.

Two: Always be sure you are well groomed. Even the best-selected outfit will not impress an interviewer if your general grooming is unacceptable. Before an interview, go over this check list:

- Is your hair clean, combed, and styled appropriately?
- Are your fingernails clean and trimmed?
- If you wear a beard or mustache, is it clean and trimmed?
- Is your perfume or aftershave lightly applied?
- Is your make-up sparingly applied?
- Have you attended to your personal hygiene (clean body, brushed teeth, etc.)?
- Have you used a deodorant?

Three: Always prepare in advance to look your best. Lay out all your clothes the night before the interview so that no last minute panic situations will occur in this regard. Plan to arrive at the interview location a few minutes early so that you can visit the washroom to check your appearance. Washing your hands and applying fresh make-up or straightening your tie will give you the fresh, clean look you want. Do it—it works!

Act Positively

Now let's go over that list of other important "dos" for interview behavior. Here are the positive factors to emphasize:

- **Do know something about the company:** It's a good idea to be able to comment about the company's products, service, and history. By doing some homework in this area, you can show the interviewer that you are really *interested* in the company. The information you need can be obtained from the business reference section of your library. However, a much simpler method is to decide on a few questions, telephone the company, and obtain the answers you want from the manager's administrative assistant. You'll usually find that the person employed in this position will be very receptive to your inquiries.

- **Do extend your hand to greet the interviewer:** Shaking hands is a polite and assertive action. It tells the interviewer that you have initiative which will probably show in your work habits.

- **Do have relevant questions to ask:** Be prepared with a list of several questions that are appropriate for the first interview. These questions should deal directly with the responsibilities of the job and with the business plan of the company. Don't try and memorize your questions. Write them down and take them with you in your portfolio.

- **Do use simple everyday words and be yourself:** Portraying someone you're not is an act you cannot possibly keep up indefinitely. By using long words from the dictionary, you run the risk of choosing an incorrect word or of having the interviewer not understand you. Be yourself!

- **Do sit up and lean into the interview:** Good body language is a *must*. It not only helps to make a good impression on the interviewer, but also helps to personally motivate *you* in the delivery of your ''sales pitch'' about your skills and special qualities.

- **Do be polite in every situation:** You may encounter interviews and situations you dislike but never let them make you rude. If you are *really* uncomfortable in an interview or have completely lost interest in the position, then politely terminate the conversation. Thank the interviewer for spending time with you and excuse yourself from the meeting. Being polite pays off as you never know when you might meet that interviewer somewhere else, or when you might wish to approach that company again.

- **Do answer every question clearly:** Some interviewers may confuse you by the questions they ask. When you are asked a confusing question, try your best to clarify the matter and then give your answer. If you cannot give an answer to a fact-finding question, then say so. Lying or making up answers may backfire on you and you will be dropped from the competition.

- **Do look for signs of withdrawal by the interviewer:** Are your answers too long or too boring? If the interviewer is "pulling away" from the interview, quickly finish your answer to the current question and be quiet. Soon, the next question will be asked and the pace of the interview will pick up again.

- **Do ask for the job:** If you want the position and feel you have the qualifications for it, then show your feelings and desires and ask for the job. Most people haven't got the nerve. But why not? By asking for the job, you'll find out how far the recruitment process has proceeded. You'll also find out just what your own chances are of obtaining the position. So do overcome your shyness and speak up. It sometimes happens that the interviewer will give the job to the first qualified candidate who asks for it!

- **Do say thank you and remember to shake hands:** A handshake is a good way to end the interview on a positive note. It not only shows good manners and confidence but also can be a good morale booster for yourself.

- **Do make notes and keep a record of the interview:** Keeping notes is always a good business practice. These notes will help you to analyze your interview skills in preparation for other interviews. Also, keeping notes on what was said by the interviewer regarding the "next step" in the process is far better than relying on your memory. You might just forget to phone or return at the time required and so lose your chance for the job.

- **Do send a thank-you note after the interview:** Surprisingly, this is a practice few people follow; yet it can be a very wise move. In a short letter, you can thank the interviewer for spending time with you. You can also introduce one more "hook" into your campaign. Now that you have all the information about the position, you can use your thank-you note to assure the interviewer that you will be able to do the job well. This will highlight another asset you possess—your ability to follow through on projects. Putting away your letter will also require the interviewer to pull out your file; and this may prompt the interviewer to take another glance at your résumé. So a thank-you note can't hurt—and it may just give you the extra edge you need to come out a winner from the interview.

Interview Questions

It's impossible to list *every* question that could be asked at an interview. Nevertheless, most interviews do follow the same general pattern and certain standard questions are often asked. A general list of such questions will be given a little further on in this section. First, however, let's deal with one specific kind of question that's regrettably often part of an interviewer's standard set—the question that may demand a negative answer.

Avoiding Negative Answers

Whenever you answer questions at an interview, you should always be careful never to introduce anything negative. Unfortunately, interviewers sometimes deliberately try to *pressure* you into giving negative information. To do this, they ask questions that may demand negative answers. If you *provide* any negative information about yourself, many interviewers will then reject your application without fully exploring your assets or positive characteristics. Yet what can you do? When you're asked a question, you have to give an honest answer. As you can see, this situation can be a problem!

The solution is to come up with a *positive* response to every question asking for negative information. To do this, you have to take things that might be considered weaknesses and present them as strengths. Such an approach will usually work. Sometimes, however, an interviewer may insist that you come straight out with any negative information in plain language, without trying to make it sound better. In this case, your only choice is to provide the information if it exists. However, *don't overdo it!* Of course, if you *don't* have anything negative to reveal, then speak up confidently with an honest answer stressing your positive qualities.

The two examples below show how to concentrate on strengths rather than weaknesses when answering questions that ask for negative information. Notice how the applicant has stressed a strength—being a fast learner—in the first example here:

- **Interviewer:** "What are your weaknesses?"
- **Applicant:** "Well, some people call my curiosity a weakness but, personally, I see it as a strength. I'm always eager to find out about things and this makes me very quick at learning all the details involved in my job."

In this next example, look at the way the applicant has avoided giving the negative information requested and has introduced the strengths of maturity and good judgment instead:

- **Interviewer:** "How old are you?"
- **Applicant:** "People always consider me very mature. I'm confident that the maturity and good judgment I show in dealing with my responsibilities will be very helpful in the position we're discussing."

Answering Standard Questions

Most interviewers have a standard set of questions. Some of these questions are fact-finding, while others are intended to calm your jitters and get you talking. A list of such questions is given below. As a practice exercise for yourself, read through these questions and write a short reply to each one.

Make your answers simple and brief. Don't wander off into side issues but keep to each question. Don't answer one question with another question. Doing so is poor strategy which may frustrate an interviewer and make a bad impression. Above all, avoid negative answers and reply positively to all questions. With these points in mind, try your hand at answering the following:

- Can you tell me something about yourself?
- Have you ever worked in this area before?
- Why do you want to work here?
- Why did you leave your last job?
- What is your present salary?
- Why did you select the college you attended?
- How long will it take you to learn this job?
- Why have you changed jobs so many times?
- What would your last boss name as the area where you need improvement?
- Why did you select the courses you took at school?
- What was your major weakness in your last job?
- How long are you planning to stay in this job?
- Can you give an example of how creative you are?
- What do you do away from the work place?
- Why didn't you finish school or continue with your education?
- What kind of salary do you need?
- Why should we hire you instead of someone else?
- How much time did you miss from your last job?
- When are you available for work?
- Are you a leader? If so, can you give me an example?
- What are your greatest strengths?
- What four words best describe you?

- What was your last employer's opinion of you?
- What are your goals for the next ten years?
- Can you work under pressure or tight deadlines?
- Do you have any questions?

Using Examples in Your Answers

By answering a question with a short example or a little story, you will help the interviewer to remember your answer. When you have something important to tell that you want the interviewer to remember, try the story-response technique. It works!

This technique is illustrated below by some questions and answers from interviews for two different positions—department supervisor and sporting goods salesclerk. For both interviews, the responses of the applicants—Marika Janic and Bart Girard—are briefly analyzed to point out how effective it can be to use little stories when answering questions. Study these examples and then practice the story-response technique yourself, in preparation for your own interviews.

Interview One: Department Supervisor

- **Interviewer:** "Do you train new staff, Marika?"
- **Applicant:** "Yes, I certainly do. Just this Monday, I started training a new person to help with the completion of an accounts payable summary report. The system I use to train new people is fairly simple. Firstly, I explain the procedure used and demonstrate by actually doing a piece of the work myself. Secondly, I ask the new person to repeat the procedure to me and to do a piece of the work while I watch. If the new person makes any errors, I point them out. Finally, I let the new person take over the job. My system works every time."

With this little story, Marika has not only answered the question but has told the interviewer that she has a system, that her system works, and that she has used it recently.

- **Interviewer:** "Marika, how many people have you hired this year?"
- **Applicant:** "Since I do all the non-management hiring for the office workers and the drivers, I would say that this year I've hired about eight people. I hired the last person about two weeks ago, just after I completed a two-day professional workshop on recruitment. It was an interesting experience to hire this person as I had an opportunity to use the skills and systems taught at the course. With the experience I have had in working with people and

the systems I now know from the workshop, I would rate myself as an interviewer who deals in facts related to the job. This is one of my many strengths.''

By telling this story, Marika has illustrated her qualifications in this area as part of her answer. Her interest in taking additional educational courses and her confidence in what she has learned certainly show her assertiveness and her desire to succeed.

Interview Two: Sporting Goods Salesclerk

- **Interviewer:** ''Bart, why do you want to work at this store?''
- **Applicant:** ''For the past four years while I've been a member of the community center squash club, I've purchased all of my supplies at this store. Last fall when I bought the prizes for the playoffs, this store gift-wrapped the prizes with special paper without being asked. I thought this was very considerate and I would like to work for a company that thinks this much of their customers.''

Through this story, Bart reveals that he is a regular and satisfied customer of the store—a fact that will probably please the interviewer. Bart's complimentary remarks about store policy are also likely to make a good impression.

- **Interviewer:** ''For this salesclerk opening, we want to hire someone with the potential to become an assistant to Mr. Marchand, the department supervisor. We want someone who can be trained to help Mr. Marchand organize work schedules and stock shipments. Are you a good organizer, Bart?''
- **Applicant:** ''Yes, I'm a very good organizer. If you call Mr. Bleam, my music teacher at school, he can tell you about the time I organized all the travel arrangements for sending our school band with their instruments to another city for a competition. I had everything so well planned and organized that I received a special thank-you letter from the principal, Ms. Waring. She complimented me on the great job I did and said that the success of the group's trip was the result of my efforts.''

Instead of simply answering ''yes'' or ''no'' to the interviewer's question, Bart expanded on his answer with an interesting little story. Bart not only answered ''yes'' he *stressed* his answer by repeating the word ''organizer'' and giving an example. He also provided the names of two other people who could confirm the fact that he had organizing skills. By using the story-response technique, Bart showed that he had that ''little bit extra'' which makes an applicant a winner.

Interview Rules

There are a few basic rules to follow to help ensure the interview will be a success. These rules shouldn't be taken lightly! Many people fail at the interview stage of their job search because they think ''luck'' is the only factor involved in winning at interviews. The fact is that successful interviews require careful planning. The rules given below provide you with information on the essential planning that's needed. Read these rules carefully so that you can observe them yourself when you go for interviews.

Be Prepared

The first rule is this. *Be prepared for the interview*. Being prepared means:

- Knowing the location of the interview
- Knowing how long it will take you to travel there
- Knowing something about the company
- Knowing whom you are going to see
- Knowing the information you want to give
- Knowing the questions you want to ask
- Knowing what you're going to wear and having it ready the day before
- Having additional copies of your résumé
- Having original reference letters plus copies
- Having original school records plus copies
- Practicing your answers to those interview questions which have caused you difficulty before
- Being emotionally prepared and motivated for a rewarding and exciting meeting

Give Proofs of Performance

Here's the second rule. *Bring proofs of performance with you to the interview*. Proofs of performance are your records of achievements either at your present or previous jobs or at school. If you are applying for a position such as draftsperson, artist, designer, etc., then bring samples of your work to the interview. Review these samples the day before and practice the way you want to present them.

Provide References

This is the final rule. *Bring a list of references to the interview.* If you haven't already provided names of references, you most certainly will be asked to do so during the interview. On a page separate from your résumé, have ready a list of business and character references who have agreed to give you a recommendation.

In selecting a reference, ask yourself whether the background of the person you have in mind relates to the line of work or the industry in which you're trying to secure employment. Also ask yourself what this person is likely to say about you. On a scale of 1-10, how will this person rate you as an individual in today's society and as a worker in today's work force?

Whomever you select, tell the person about the job for which you are applying, why you want this job, and why you think your background or education will help you to do this job. It certainly makes a good impression on an interviewer when a reference reaffirms the same positive information you gave during the interview.

10

Starting Your New Job

10 Starting Your New Job

Congratulations—you're hired! Using this book's proven system, you've found your ideal job and you're ready to start work. Now this chapter has some very important recommendations about bringing your whole job search program to a happy conclusion.

Succeed as an Employee

Everyone will be waiting to see YOU, the new employee. First impressions were important at the interview and they are equally important on your first day at work. The manager or interviewer who hired you will have told some of your co-workers about your good appearance and your positive personal characteristics. Don't destroy that image! Poor impressions can take months to change and may have a serious effect on your probation period. Now that you have the right job, you want to succeed at it. The following list of suggestions will help you to do so.

1. Arrive ten minutes early on your first day—no more and no less. If you arrive *too* early, you may find you're the only one there. Being late is *not acceptable*.
2. Dress conservatively and appropriately for the job. If you've received instructions about dress, follow them. If you're not sure about what to wear, ask the interviewer or observe the other employees coming out of the building. Your personal appearance will make a first impression that will last indefinitely.
3. Listen, observe, and write down information. Don't be shy about asking questions. That first day is difficult. Since your memory is being used to its limits, assist it by keeping notes on a small pad and reviewing them when you get home.
4. Use your first day to obtain information about parking, lunch hour, coffee breaks, and who's who. If you smoke, observe company rules and regulations. Parking in the spot reserved for the boss, or thinking that the company president is one of the part-time workers does not help employee/employer relations. Some companies will provide information about all these matters during an orientation lecture, but many leave it up to you to learn the system.

5. Use the phone for business only. Family and friends may be anxious about your first day; however, they should not call you at work to inquire how things are going. Your boss and co-workers will be aware of your personal use of the phone and you will find it embarrassing if you have to be reminded that the phone is for business.

6. Establish a goal to have perfect attendance and excellent work habits. Your employer has hired you on the assumption that you will be an asset to the firm. Don't let your new boss down. Employers want regular attendance. They also want your work to be done according to the high standards that will live up to their expectations. Meet these requirements and you will have no problems with your new job.

7. Make it your policy to always be polite and well-mannered at work. Even though there may be times when you will be tempted to let off steam, remember that it takes more character to remain calm and polite than to blow up and say things you may regret. It may be difficult to keep your temper at times, but you will be respected for your self-control.

8. Put yourself in the employer's shoes for a moment to help you understand the kind of job performance your boss expects. If your attitude towards your job is positive and mature, and if you work hard and learn everything you can, you will be a successful employee.

Conclude Your Program

Now that you're happily settled in your new job, it's time to close down your job search program.

Get in touch with your network of contact people and thank them for their help. Share your enthusiasm about your new job with your contacts. If they were concerned enough to help you, they will be interested in hearing about your job. If you have any other applications still active on the job market, contact these employers by phone or mail. Explain that you have accepted another job and thank the employers for their time and consideration.

Closing down your system in this prompt and professional manner is a gesture that will be appreciated by all parties. By showing this courtesy, you'll ensure that the doors will always swing open again, whenever you need to use your system in the future.

Stairway to Success

All the different parts of the job search system described in this book form a stairway leading to the one goal—your ideal job. Each new step on this stairway is built on the step that came before it. You can't climb the stairway successfully unless you cover each step on the way.

Good managers keep a record of their progress on projects or assignments for which they are responsible. Your job search project must be handled in the same way. *You* are the manager of this project! It's important to keep track of your progress and check to make sure you haven't left out any of the steps in the system.

To help you do this, use the personal chart, *My System Check List,* provided on page 109. As you cover each step on the stairway, fill in the "Date Completed" column on your chart. By the time you write the last date on the chart, you will have accomplished your goal, reached the top of the stairway, and achieved success: meaningful employment. Happy job hunting!

My System Check List

My Job Search Goal _____

Steps towards Goal	See Chapter	Date Completed
• Set up my own home office with the necessary supplies and equipment	1	_____
• Understand what employers expect from employees	2	_____
• Identify my own top strengths	2	_____
• Identify my own main skills	2	_____
• Prepare my positive résumé that will attract the reader's interest	3	_____
• Practice writing effective covering letters to accompany my résumé	3	_____
• Prepare my information card	3	_____
• Discover the ''networking secret''	4	_____
• Make up my list of contact people	4	_____
• Set up my contacts file	4	_____
• Set up my job leads file	5	_____
• Understand how to make the best use of job advertisements and agencies	5	_____
• Understand how to find clues to job leads in directories, magazines, and trade journals	5	_____
• Define my general expectations as an employee	6	_____
• Identify what working conditions I do not want in my ideal job	6	_____
• Draw up a realistic personal budget as a guide to my net pay requirements	6	_____
• Identify the techniques required for making effective phone calls to employers	7	_____
• Understand how to continually pull new leads back into my job search system	7	_____
• Identify the techniques required for writing effective letters in answer to advertisements	8	_____
• Understand the ''dos'' and ''don'ts'' involved in handling interviews effectively	9	_____
• Identify the techniques required for giving effective answers to interview questions	9	_____
• Understand the rules for successful interviews	9	_____
• Understand how to succeed as an employee	10	_____
• Close down my job search program	10	_____